EARLY YEARS SUMMIT

Personal, Social and Emotional Well-being in Young Children

Kathy Brodie et al.

ISBN: 978-0992763121
Rainmaker Publishing, Wilmslow, SK9 3AH

DEDICATION

For Ian, Chris and Robs

CONTENTS

ACKNOWLEDGEMENTS   vii

ABOUT THE AUTHOR

INTRODUCTION   ix
The Early Years Web Summit

1   CHILDREN'S INDEPENDENCE AND SELF-REGULATION   1
Marion Dowling

2   HOW CAN WE RECOGNISE AND REDUCE ANXIETY IN   17
YOUNG CHILDREN
Jane Evans

3   THE HIGH ACHIEVING, WHITE WORKING CLASS BOYS   33
RESEARCH (HAWWC) PROJECT
Professor Chris Pascal OBE and Professor Tony Bertram

4   WHY ARE DROP-OFFS AND PICK UPS SO IMPORTANT TO A   53
CHILD'S DAY?
Suzanne Zeedyk

5   SUPPORTING THE PSED OF CHILDREN AGED BIRTH TO   83
THREE
Julia Manning-Morton

6   A MALE PRACTITIONER IN A FEMALE ENVIRONMENT   101
Rob Fox

7   THE TRANSITION FROM RECEPTION YEAR INTO YEAR ONE   109
Alistair Bryce-Clegg

8   THE PHOENIX CUPS PHILOSOPHY   135
Sandi Phoenix

9   PSED AND CHILDREN WITH AUTISM   153
Michelle Myers

10 PEDAGOGICAL DOCUMENTATION   173
    Debi Keyte-Hartland

11 CHILDREN'S MENTAL HEALTH   189
    Wendy Baker

12 THE REGGIO EMILIA APPROACH AND PSED   203
    Suzanne Axelsson

13 PRACTITIONER'S OWN WELL-BEING AND MINDFULNESS   223
    Sonia Mainstone-Cotton

14 THE PRACTICAL BENEFITS OF NEUROSCIENCE IN   239
    CHILDREN'S PSED – BEING BRAIN BUILDERS
    Mine Conkbayir

15 USING THE LEUVEN SCALES TO IMPROVE OUR PRACTICE   259
    Dr Sue Allingham

16 THE LINKS BETWEEN PHYSICAL DEVELOPMENT AND PSED   277
    Sally Goddard-Blythe

ACKNOWLEDGMENTS

This book is a collaboration that goes far beyond the pages here. Starting from the beginning: Ian Brodie cajoled and supported me in equal measure into creating my first Summit. Penny Pullan taught me the process and was incredibly generous with her expertise and insights into Summits. Navid Moazzez's excellent Virtual Summit Mastery course enabled me to develop this. The sponsors of the Summit, (iConnect, First Discoverers, PACEY, Pre-School Learning Alliance) who make it possible to offer the Summit to practitioners and educators at a realistic price.

This book would not even exist without the amazing and inspirational speakers, all of whom were very generous with their time, sharing their expertise and research results for the benefit of the whole Early Years Community around the world. Thank you one and all!

I'd like to extend my heartfelt thanks to all the Early Years people who have taken an interest in the Summit and engaged with both process and product.

Finally, my sincere gratitude to my family and friends who have endured me obsess about number of sign-up, video editing and many other aspects of Summits that I am certain were of little interest to them. I appreciate your time and patience with me.

ABOUT THE AUTHOR

Kathy Brodie has worked in the Early Years sector for 20 years, starting off as a mum who stayed at nursery, helped out at school and never wanted to leave. She has worked in a range of different settings, maintained and private, as a practitioner, Special Educational Needs Coordinator and Early Years Professional. She was awarded her Masters in Early Childhood Education at the University of Sheffield, UK.

During her time in the Early Years sector, she has had the privilege and honour to meet many inspirational children, and countless dedicated, enthusiastic adults. The online Summits are a way of bringing continued professional development to those dedicated practitioners, to help them to support and educate all the amazing children in their care.

INTRODUCTION

The Spring 2017 Early Years Web Summit was broadcast from the 20th March to the 31st of March, 2017. I chose the theme of 'children's personal, social and emotional development' after much discussion with those in the Early Years sector, including online discussions. It seems that this is still an area worthy of further debate. I was delighted at this, because I personally believe that without good personal, social and emotional development that any other type of learning is made very difficult, if not impossible.

The Summit itself is a series of interviews with 17 Early Years experts from around the world, talking about their particular specialisms. This book is a transcript of those interviews. Therefore, they are accessible explanations of, in some cases, some highly complex pedagogical concepts and theoretical frameworks, rather than a piece of academic writing. For me, this makes them very 'user-friendly'. Rather than dense, heavily referenced text books, these are experts following a thread of thought, explaining their work with children, how they have come to their conclusions, the reasons behind their research, their personal views and unique experiences. I would urge you to follow up any areas of interest in the aforementioned text books and start to reflect on what this means to your practice, wherever you are in the world.

The interviews cover a wide breadth and depth of subjects around this incredibly complex area, and you will see several speakers say that this is just a fraction of a fraction their specialism. This is certainly not a definitive answer to all questions about children's personal, social and emotion development, but I hope it will give you plenty to reflect on and apply to your practice.

Finally, every speaker is asked about practical strategies (or top tips) for applying their theories to your work with children. I felt this was exceptionally important. After all, this is all about ensuring the very best for the children in our care.

Notes on abbreviations

Ofsted - is the Office for Standards in Education, Children's Services and Skills, who inspect and regulate services that care for children and young people.

EYFS – is the Early Years Foundation Stage, the English curriculum for children aged birth to five.

SENCO – stands for Special Educational Needs Co-ordinator and is the person who specialises in Special Educational Needs in the setting

Characteristics of Effective Learning – are a non-statutory, set of supporting concepts about elements of children's learning

Prime Areas of the EYFS – The three areas of learning and development that the EYFS identifies as being 'prime' to children's development. They are: personal, social and emotional; physical development; communication and language.

Two year old progress check – A statutory part of the EYFS, which requires parents and carers have a short written summary of their child's development in the three Prime areas, when their child is between 24 months and 36 months old.

Key Stage One – the academic stage that follows the EYFS

- Kathy Brodie, March 2017

CHAPTER 1

CHILDREN'S INDEPENDENCE AND SELF-REGULATION

Marion Dowling

Kathy Brodie: Marion Dowling needs little introduction in the world of children's personal, social and emotional development. Her fantastic book 'Young Children's Personal, Social and Emotional development' available from Sage publications, is now in its fourth edition and it's still my 'go to' book whenever I do anything about children's PSED. It's just a fantastic book linked with loads of theory and practice.

Marion also leads training and keynotes at conferences on children's personal, social, emotional development, as well as many other aspects of children's development - and certainly whenever I've seen her, she's always done that to great acclaim and the sorts of comments that we get are inspirational, supportive and thought provoking.

I'm absolutely delighted that Marion has been able to join us today on the Early Years Web Summit all about personal, social and emotional development. Welcome to the Early Years Web Summit Marion Dowling.

Marion Dowling: Thank you, Kathy. Do you know it's a real pleasure to take part in this Summit, because PSED is very close to my heart and as a nursery head teacher said to me, some years ago now, "our job here is to nurture children, but also to help grow the adequate person". And I absolutely agree with her.

Kathy Brodie: Yes absolutely. It's such a bedrock of children's development isn't it? And that's a lovely way to put it as well.

PSED is a massive topic. It covers so many areas of children's development, so today we're just going to focus on two specific areas - children's independence and children's self-regulation. Would you like to just give us a brief introduction, first of all, as to what we mean by children's independence and how you would see that in children, and maybe where that sits with the UK government?

Marion Dowling: Thank you Kathy. Just let me continue with this notion of adequacy, because I think it's fundamental really and most of us would recognise an adequate person - somebody who can relate easily to other people, good interpersonal skills and live their lives by a clear moral code, and can handle their feelings and also empathize the feelings of others.

I think that sort of person, when difficulties come along in life, as they do, they face them bravely and make decisions clearly. These people very often are full of vigour and a good sense of humour, which is important regardless of their intellectual capacities. These people seem equipped to lead their lives fully and also to deal with problems. Now, that's a very rough and ready description of adequacy, I know, but I hope that you would agree with me, all of you, that really we need to nurture, recognise and promote these qualities in young children. Young children are growing up in the spring time of their lives and there's everything to play for, their growth is embryonic. And so the young baby waits for us to give our messages, he responds and he takes our nurture.

Kathy Brodie: And as you say, that is from babyhood, it's right from babe in our arms.

Marion Dowling: Yes it is. So, moving on to independence. I think you said originally, you asked if it was the priority of governments. Well, I think they would like to say "yes it is and we demonstrate that". I have severe reservations about that. We live in a very controlling culture, very competitive as well. And this is coupled with our young children being urged to achieve as much as possible, as early as possible. I think people recognize that now, parents and some practitioners, and they see this as an opportunity to urge their young children to accelerate their learning, particularly in mathematics and literacy. But, you and I know that achievement is much broader than this. That's really why I've decided to look at independence and self-regulation because I think they're absolutely basic to development.

Kathy Brodie: So could you describe for me what being independent would look like in a child, what would a practitioner recognize in a child as then being independent?

Marion Dowling: Well all, practitioners, I believe, think that independence is important. That's a given. But there are many different understandings of this. Just two broad headings. Some people would say the most important thing is for a child to make a good transition from parents, separate happily from parents, particularly when they going into a nursery environment or if they're actually going to a childminder even. Also, to attend to their personal needs - going to the toilet unaided, learning to wash themselves and indeed feed themselves and dress themselves. So those, I think, are given a high profile. Other people would say look, surely the priority is for young children to learn to think for themselves. Now, in fact, all of these aspects are important for independence, they all come together really. And it's just terribly important that all of us recognize that babyhood is the start of independence. Young babies make decisions about what they want to eat, what they want to play with and actually whose company they prefer. Given an enabling environment, babies really do thrive in starting to make decisions for themselves.

Kathy Brodie: I think that's such a good point. We often think about independence as being that pre-school skill, ready to go to school. As you say, babies make choices as well, don't they? They can be very vocal about their choices! Their independence really starts from that that babyhood. And it covers such a wide range of things doesn't it.

Marion Dowling: Yes it does. And one example of this: One of the inhibitors I think of independence is when children are overprotected. That is a factor, with some children and some parents and even key persons - with key persons they tend to over protect children.

Let me just talk about Alise for a moment because I met this child and I met her parents and, a lovely little girl of two, very loving parents, an only child. Alise was very well cared for, but the parents never allowed Alise to go outside, unless she was on a rein and indoors, she was never allowed to climb a stair, let alone a staircase. She was always carried. This was continuing so, at three and a half, she started in my nursery school. The workforce, the people there, gently tried to persuade the parents to allow Alise a little more flexibility, a little more freedom. But, by that time Alise, at three and a half, her movements were very tentative and she was very, very reluctant to take the smallest risk and this continued. Now I thought, these parents want the best for Alise, but they've never allowed her to learn through trial and error and really by four, even if we look at Alise her physical development and her level of confidence were delayed.

Kathy Brodie: But as you say the parents are trying to do the very best for their child. And they think that they're doing that by keeping her safe. But by not giving it the independence that is that's going to be detrimental. And that's really interesting. That's not just about personal, social and emotional development, that's going to be physical development, that's going to have manifestations in all areas of learning and development. What a good example.

Marion Dowling: I think we have to look out for that. So loving parents can feel they're doing the best but that doesn't always happen, does it really?

Kathy Brodie: Have you any top tips and strategies for practitioners in developing independence. We've identified that it is so important, so what sorts of things can practitioners do? You've already identified they've got to be supportive with the children that they've got coming in and they've identified that there's an extra need there. What are the sorts of things can practitioners do to support children's independence ?

Marion Dowling: Well I do think giving them scope to make decisions for themselves. If we look at an environment for example. An environment - they can't always be spacious - but to be equipped with continuous provision, the same resources out day after day. The quality of continuous provision has a huge impact on children's play but this allows them to make choices, so I think that's very important. And for children to become independent, they need to feel in control of things and I think having a predictable program, particularly for very young children and new children. It is important to have a visual timeline, which helps children because they can actually see time passing, particularly if there are little items that could be removed from the line. So we've had registration now and then we're going to have choosing time or whatever you like to call it. So that gives them a sense of security and makes them feel what they *do* know what's coming next, rather than being in a complete fog about whatever is in the hands of the adult.

Kathy Brodie: Yes, absolutely. As adults we like that, if we're going to a conference or if we are going out somewhere, we like to know what time we've got to be there, when's break, we need to know that.

Marion Dowling: So it is a matter of giving children information, its really important. But I'll come back to a couple of those points later on.

Kathy Brodie: Interesting. So can we just move on then to self-regulation. Could you give us a little explanation of what self-regulation actually is and why that is so important, why you've chosen to talk about that today please.

Marion Dowling: Yes. Well, I decided on this because we hear more and more that of that term and we didn't in the past. What exactly does it mean? I think people use it without really understanding. It's quite similar to independence.

Those of us who are self regulated, and there are gaps in self regulation of adults as well as children, but those of us who are, are in control of our feelings our behaviour and our learning and we're in control rather than being controlled. That's the most important aspect I think.

Why is it so important? Well, it is quite difficult to actually describe this because it wasn't a term that was always used. But we do need to get children to restrain their impulses. We all know of adults who are very impulsive. If we are hostage to our impulses and emotions, it makes it much more difficult for us to persevere and concentrate on things. I think harnessing our impulses is tremendously important. Stop doing something, for instance, that we like doing and do something we know we *have* to do - and translate it for a young child. If they're playing in role play and enjoying it, but they know full well that the session is coming to an end, then it is time to clear up, that is necessary. Now that's where you see at an early age self-regulation coming in because some children will immediately go ahead and do that. They know what's necessary and others tend to ignore you.

Good old Brigitte Plowden in 1964, she coined a wonderful phrase, she said "children should be agents in their own learning". Of course, that just encapsulates one of the main elements of self-regulation. Being in charge or managing your learning in the

Sixties was beginning to be seen as being important, although there was still a lot of control.

Today I believe it's imperative because our children are growing up in a world where there are no certainties. And so they need to be flexible and adapt. They do need to make thoughtful and informed choices. And that sounds very grand for young children, but it's a beginning. We need to encourage those sorts of things because, to a large extent, these children are going to be in charge of their own destinies.

Kathy Brodie: More so than ever in history really aren't they?

Marion Dowling: Absolutely right. And we must be quite clear that there's a huge difference now between self-regulation and compliancy. In the past, compliancy was recognized and highlighted as a good thing. If children followed the instructions of adults, if their behaviour was compliant and, basically, they did as they were told, they were regarded as good pupils and will probably do well in life. Nowadays we can see that it can lead to a culture of dependency and really children don't have the opportunity, in that culture, to think and learn for themselves and that's what we really want to get to.

I just want to take a little look at the characteristics of effective learning. Well, it's one of my favourite parts of The Early Years Foundation Stage, it really does chime with us. I'm sure everybody watching this will be very familiar with the three characteristics:

1. Playing and exploring; children engaged as agents in their own learning - so there's Plowden being echoed;

2. Active learning, children motivated to learn, hungry to learn, curious, asking questions. And that's such a driver isn't it? Because without that motivation, we can't go anywhere. We can't *make* children learn so we

can harness the motivation that takes some skill sometimes.

3. And finally the third one, creating and thinking critically, having their own ideas. Yes, being given ideas, but actually making them their own, personalizing learning, making links in those things. So thinking to themselves "yes... that little dog in the story we had today, that's like my grandma's dog at home". So making those links between certain things and then choosing ways to do things.

So all of these three aspects are distinct but they can all come together and together they really do contribute strongly to self regulation.

Kathy Brodie: You need to have that sense of self regulation, to have the critical thinking, to have that curiosity to continue to investigate. You don't just give up at the first opportunity and walk away from it.

Marion Dowling: I think it's rather a pity that term wasn't used in the Early Years Foundation Stage, but there we are. When we actually unpick the elements, they're all there to promote this.

Kathy Brodie: In some respects this isn't a new idea, this hasn't just come in with it 2008 EYFS, theorists have been talking about types of self regulation for a number of years haven't they? So could you take us through a couple of theories that maybe this is grounded in please?

Marion Dowling: Yes, I'm glad you said that because, in fact, it isn't a new idea although the term itself is quite new.

Let me just start very briefly with Piaget, who sometimes is discredited these days. But, you know he was an educational giant in his time. One of the things that Piaget stated strongly was that children don't learn things by being told. He saw them as little scientists and our job, which we would see much wider now, he sees the adult job as providing those experiences that children can make sense of, in order to move on in their learning. So that's Piaget.

Two others who I think are very important are Vygotsky and Bruner. Now both of these eminent psychologists, believe strongly that learning was social. We didn't learn by ourselves - we learned with other people. And Vygotsky is famously known for saying 'what a child does in cooperation with others today, he will eventually learn to do for himself'. I think that's a paraphrase but that was the sense of his message! Vygotsky introduced the ZPD, the Zone of Proximal Development, which always sounds very technical. Actually, it's the gap between what children know and are in independent in doing and the proximal step, the next step, in learning that they must take. And that to me is tremendously important because it does highlight the need for very close observation of children and then that informed guess as to what comes next.

Bruner did agree with Vygotsky, he took on board a lot of his notions, but very usefully went a step further and actually introduced scaffolding - a way that adults can support young children. The great thing about scaffolding is that it's bespoke to every child. So one child might need a very light scaffold to help them move on, lasting for a very brief period of time. Others might need a more substantial scaffold to actually give them time to move on to quite a big gap in their learning and then eventually they will be independent. When they're independent, when they are self regulated, the scaffold is removed.

I don't believe we can teach self-regulation. I don't think there's a lesson that will teach it, but what we can do is follow the theories of these eminent people and apply some of the notions, the Zone of Proximal Development and the emphasis on really looking at children closely and scaffolding and we can scaffold their development in every day activities.

Kathy Brodie: For me, scaffolding is such a great phrase because visually, it's a lovely image. And the idea that some of them are going to be more permanent than others. It is a total solution, you're not just spoon feeding the answer. This is something you're supporting them and you're expecting to step away and, of course, that links very closely with that idea of independence - that's what you're giving in that independence afterwards.

Marion Dowling: That's what we're working for. Yes it is.

Kathy Brodie: You don't think we can't actually teach self-regulation. But there must be some strategies or some top tips that maybe practitioners could put in to practice to help self-regulation.

Marion Dowling: Let me just give you an example. Turn to physical development. I think physical development is quite a useful one to expand on, because we're very aware now, we've been made very aware, of the importance of physical development - forest schools, children being active to stop obesity, all that sort of thing. But we are not quite so sure about the benefits of self regulation that physical development would need. In physical play, given the opportunity, children will set goals for themselves. That's the important one. They're in control and they've developed the strategy or strategies for achieving that goal. A simple example, just balancing along the plank. Stand up straight and look straight ahead. Okay. They then persevere in those actions and they're very aware of when they succeed, or indeed, when they fail. But undaunted, they will persevere and try again. Why is this? Because again, it's their own goal. They're not required to do it. They're setting their own goals. So they try again, they persevere. And it's that drive to achieve competence. And also I think to be in control of your own body. And that's a very heady feeling, for all of us really isn't it? I think that it's very useful to look at self regulation being exhibited through physical play.

We can provide good support for this. I think it's a very straightforward really. One of the main things - and just keeping to this balancing example - we're available and we're interested, no more than that. We're not being intrusive, we're not telling them how to do things, but we are **there**. All this needs is body language, it doesn't need any words really - a thumbs up, a big smile, a big nod to show them that we're there and we really are encouraging and being affirmative. I think this is probably the most important.

Encouraging the child to struggle though, so he keeps falling off this plank, is beginning to get disheartened, so you'd say "just try one more time" and then maybe a gentle suggestion, but it's not telling him to do it, just a little bit of advice, maybe. "Well perhaps if you move a little more slowly, you can put one foot in front of the other and move a little more slowly". He can reject that but it's just a suggestion. And then what you're doing is sensitively withdrawing support when you see he's achieved. Because what you been offering him is a form of light scaffold. And you can demonstrate when you feel 'Yes he's there. He's achieved his goal' with a thumbs up and a nod and maybe a "Well done!" Then you turn your attention to all of the children that need you! But most importantly Kathy, I think is that at all times you're allowing the child to make the decision about what he's doing. You're not taking over at all.

Kathy Brodie: If I've understood this correctly, that's throughout every activity. That's a constant, almost philosophy, of supporting children rather than stepping in and telling them how to do it or taking over their activities and just saying all "This is how you must do it. This is the one way, the one right way to do things". Am I right in that?

Marion Dowling: Yes I do think that practitioners, who to my mind are wonderful people and they work so hard, but there is a tendency to take over and to show them the way because we know better. They would be horrified, actually I think, realizing that that's the case. It's a matter of standing back and letting the child grow themselves.

Kathy Brodie: It is very difficult to stand back and do that sometimes, if you see a child struggling or you think, if he just turns that jigsaw piece round he'll get that, and you really do have to hold yourself back down.

Marion Dowling: Yes, you do. So that requires your own self regulation, doesn't it really? You're restraining your impulses. You know it's something that could apply in so many cases, really.

Kathy Brodie: And I think that maybe that is another top tip for practitioners - just have a look at your own self regulation. Do you always jump in? Maybe hold a mirror up to your own practice as well, which is good reflective practice anyway. What would your top tip be, your biggest tip for practitioners when they're trying to encourage children's self-regulation?

Marion Dowling: I would say to them, quite a lot has been offered today. But when you get back to your room and you've had a session just ask yourself "how much have I done today that young children could have done equally well for themselves?".

Now obviously we can't allow children to make all the decisions. Tina Bruce once said, quite rightly, at times the adult must lead and at times the child. But I do think it's a very good question because if you're honest you can identify when you've perhaps taken over, done too much. Children haven't got enough responsibility. Now if they haven't got enough responsibility that can lead to a bit of disaffection with poor behaviour. So we want to respect their ability to do as much for themselves as they can and step up a little.

Kathy Brodie: Yes I think that respect is really core to that, as well isn't it? Just to have that bit of respect and maybe a little bit of trust that they will get there eventually. It might not be to our timescales but they will get there in their own time scales.

Marion Dowling: What they learned as a result. The important thing is what the child has learned.

Kathy Brodie: As adults, we're the same. We don't pick things up straight away, we have to have two or three goes at things and everything we learn, we usually have to do that, so children aren't going to be a lot different from that, are they?

So we've looked at independence and we've looked at self-regulation and we've seen that there's quite a lot of overlap in there. If there is something that practitioners can do, just one thing, that practitioners could implement tomorrow morning when they go into their setting. What would your one thing be to help children in their independence and self regulation and personal, social and emotional development?

Marion Dowling: Well I would say, we have to make sure that children have this 'I can' approach. I'm really offering a couple of suggestions here. You need to be very sure about those children who we call the 'silent children'. The ones we don't know enough about, those who are very tentative. How are we going to help them feel 'I can'? It's a very, very slow process, but I think you have to have that in mind going into your classroom.

The other one is really to do with looking around the room,

before the children come in. You've been very careful with the layout. It looks beautiful and very well organized. How much is there here in my setting, in these activities, to really enthuse children to think for themselves and have some intellectual challenge?

Kathy Brodie: I think that's lovely. Those few quiet moments before the children arrive, and as you say, just look around and see everything's there. That would be a great little question just to have on the back of the staffroom door as they leave. "Just have a look at your environment and think - Is this challenging the children?"

Thank you very, very much indeed Marion Dowling. As always, a great pleasure to talk with you especially about PSED. This is my favourite book on PSED. I highly recommend it to anybody. And thank you very much indeed to our viewers and listeners today for joining us on the Early Years Web Summit.

Marion Dowling: Thank you. Kathy it's been a pleasure.

CHAPTER 2

HOW CAN WE RECOGNISE AND REDUCE ANXIETY IN YOUNG CHILDREN

Jane Evans

Kathy Brodie: I'm very excited to be joined by Jane Evans. Jane started working in Early Years in education twenty two years ago as a supervisor in a pre-school and she loved it. She also worked at a pre-school with children who had complex physical learning and emotional needs and was a childminder. The children taught her so much and encouraged her to study their development and needs, so she could better support and care for them. Jane now regularly delivers training to Early Years settings and speaks at conferences all over the world focussing on the impact of childhood trauma and anxiety in Early Years development. Welcome to the Web Summit Jane Evans.

Jane Evans: Thank you so much for having me here. I'm very excited to be with you.

Kathy Brodie: This is a really exciting area of child development. Today we're going to focus on one particular area because it's such a massive topic. And the thing we're going to look at today is anxiety in Early Years children. But first of all, please could you explain to me what is anxiety in Early Years children?

Jane Evans: Well, it's hard to believe in a way that such young children would be anxious. It is normal for us all to have moments of stress in our lives so, parting from mummy, daddy, nanny whoever brought them in, in the morning will cause a child's stress. But what we should see is within half an hour, or even sooner, that they settle into their day. And actually it's looking for changes in the body. They often come in quite tense. What you should see is that kind of relaxation and they begin to be really absorbed in what they're doing.

Now if you're *not* seeing that and you're maybe getting prolonged crying or lots of moving around the room, the body's very stiff, flitting from one thing to another, then I would be curious about why is this taking so long and be looking for what the levels of anxiety are. It expresses itself, for the child, in a very physical way but also when we're observing we should be able to notice it in the physical presentation of the child.

Kathy Brodie: So as you say, it's that sort of that physical relaxation. What other sorts of things would be a sign of anxiety in children?

Jane Evans: Okay, so things that often get labelled as bad behaviour, actually. There are many, many anxious children who get themselves in to all sorts of situations in Early Years because we perceive them as being challenging.

Unfortunately, some settings are still quite punitive and they may put in consequences for behaviour. So what we might see is things like randomly pushing the child over or that inability to settle to one thing. Maybe they have a tiny injury, you're quite sure it really was not that much, but you get this dramatic outburst - prolonged crying, can't be soothed. Presenting with eating difficulties, so they really struggle to eat their food, can't sit on a chair, seem to lack the ability to hear and experience a lot of sensory overload, so as soon as noise levels go up, they just can't cope. You might find them sitting in the corner with their hands on their ears, rocking. I could go on - really it is anything that you notice and you need to be curious about -does this comes from a place of anxiety?

Kathy Brodie: So sometimes that will be that gut reaction? "That isn't the behaviour that I'd expect from a child. That's something a bit unusual", maybe?

Jane Evans: Absolutely yes. I encourage all practitioners to be more attuned to your gut, because we have brain cells in our gut. Gut feeling is a real neurological thing, which we don't prize enough. I remember when I was a practitioner, particularly in the beginning, I wasn't very confident so I might notice things, feel things but who was I to mention it? So it's having that confidence to pass it on as a curiosity. So recently I spent a whole day just observing children in a nursery, as part of a two day training I was doing. And was able to pass on my observation that a child who spent the first half of his day running around on his tip toes. And then, because I watched him again in the afternoon, I noticed by then he was on the flats off his feet walking around. So when we were in the training the next day I said "You know, to me, that is a sign that this is a highly anxious child". It took him half a day to settle.

Kathy Brodie: And of course some children are only in the setting half a day, anyway and then they're going through the transition of leaving the setting. So that's a really interesting physical manifestation as well. That's the sort of thing you might notice, if a child was running round on their tiptoes. Do you think we are seeing an increase in anxiety in children?

Jane Evans: Most definitely yes. I mean certainly the statistics are showing that. If you visit any of the statistics in most countries, to be honest, what you're finding is mental health problems in much younger children. Unfortunately many of them get diagnosed with things that they may or may not have. And increasingly medicated, again for things that they may or may not have. And yes, if you look at the statistics globally, mental illness in never mind young people (well, we do mind young people) but very often in children is on the up and I did a TED Talk in 2015 and I put some statistics up of levels of medication in America. The American medical system is different from us but 250,000 nought to 12 month old babies are using medication for anxiety.

Kathy Brodie: That's just incredible isn't it. So do you think that's because we're now better at diagnosing that, at spotting these signs? Or do you think that's kind of in a knee jerk reaction because at that sorts out the symptoms rather than the problem?

Jane Evans: Yeah, I would said exactly that Kathy. We've got to a point now where we medicalize children. We look at them individually, we don't look at the whole package. So when I work with parents, (or I work a lot with foster carers as well and kinship carers), with as much knowledge that we have, we go right back to what was going on with the person who carried this child? Who was pregnant with this child? What was the birth like? What was after the birth like? Because there's a significant body of information. So if we just look at a child, then we can run a checklist and we can diagnose them with many things and which again, they may or may not have, but we need to start looking at the whole picture.

Kathy Brodie: Yes. Absolutely and I think we've all done that Google search, haven't we, if we felt a little bit ill ourselves and suddenly we've discover we've got all these illnesses we don't have. As you say, looking at that whole package.

So, what would your advice be to practitioners if these are sounding familiar, starting ringing a few alarm bells. What sort of things can practitioners do to support the children in their care?

Jane Evans: Well, what I advise now, which is very much founded in the latest research and neuroscience is actually it starts with us.

Kathy Brodie: As practitioners? as adults?

Jane Evans: Yes. So this for me is a very joyful thing, because we *do* have the power. The children do not. Children are completely powerless and reliant on upon us and what we bring to the table. We have the power to create environments and surround them with human beings who are well regulated human beings. I know from my own work in Early Years and in the work I still do there, that many practitioners, as in schools as well, are under immense pressure so they're showing up at work like this * Anxious face *

Kathy Brodie: They're already at that very high anxiety levels.

Jane Evans: Exactly! So, the most important thing is to look at the environment. So let's clear some of this stuff out of rooms. Many of the rooms are just an assault on the senses. Children do need stimulation, we know that. The most important stimulation is this here * indicating her facial features * and we need toys, but we don't need every toy. And we don't need every space of the wall covered in stuff. We need quiet, beautiful, really lovely simple sensory space that's simple, but that's always there, it's not a thing, it's just always there.

But the most important thing is in the morning before we go near a child * deep breath in * we check in with ourselves. We breathe. We literally ground ourselves. And then we go near a child. We don't go near a child until you've done that. Then we do this throughout the day with the children, whether they're babes in arms - even better if we're holding them - and we're breathing deeply, we're connecting to the ground. Anything we do in our physical body, the children really feel it - good or bad - because they are not so much upper brain so they're much more gut instinct to if you like.

Kathy Brodie: So they're picking up on all those nonverbal signals that we're giving as well that's all. So I know I've been to, and worked in, settings where, for example, the staff room (if they have a staff room, they don't all have staff rooms) are, again, an assault on the senses. It's quite manic in there and it's almost throw your handbag in there, get that locked up and get out there, get into your room. So are you suggesting then that maybe we should have that as part of our regular daily routine? Just have a few five minutes get a glass of water, come into work and just relax for a minute or two?

Jane Evans: Most definitely. We need leaders in Early Years who prioritize the wellness of their staff on the regulation of their staff. The point I've got to, after nearly 23 years of working with parents and children and young people, I would never go near one unless I know that I am regulated. Because I know in the past I've rushed from one thing to another, maybe I've come in, I've just had a big row with my son on the way or whatever. And you get into work and then you hear some emergency has happened and by the time you get near these little vulnerable nervous systems and vulnerable brains * highly anxious face * and you're rushing to get everything done.

The children would much prefer to have less done and have *you*. They've been grabbed out of their beds, maybe, in the morning by the poor stressed parent who's got to get somewhere. So they've had a morning of * sharp intake of breath *. And then they've had to part from the person they love the most in the universe * even deeper intake of breath *

They need to come into this warm bath. You know yourself, sometimes when you go somewhere it's like stepping into a warm bath. That's exactly what they need and they need not be put in circle time straight away, they need lots of holding, either emotionally or physically settling into the day, some breathing. And then you can think about other stuff.

Kathy Brodie: That's a really great strategy for when you start the day, but as the day goes on obviously things happen. There might be further tensions in the day. Lunchtime might not go so well then you get the changeover, and so by the end of the day we can all be sort of ready for going home and being quite fraught.

Is there anything that practitioners can do throughout the day that kind of brings that anxiety level back down for children?

Jane Evans: Most definitely. You know, again being in the nursery the other day, I'm watching the journey that children go through. Now most of the adults, not actually I have to say in this nursery, but most of the adults when it comes near lunch time * anxious face *, when it's going in the garden time... All the adults get in a stress and we had these rigid routines in some settings - not all - and the pressure to get children to eat because you have to write down what they've eaten. And now again as soon as the adults go up, then the children do too - if you see a herd of wildebeest on the television, when one goes up goes round the whole herd. Or meerkats, in my case, it would be meerkats, one goes up, they all go up. So it's throughout the day you have you have to really commit to this as a way of life for yourself. So it's every, I don't know, half an hour, just making sure we all do our big sunshine breaths. We have a stretch. We are trees that sway in the wind. We feel our toes on the ground.

It doesn't matter what the children understand but, as we know, they will copy us, good or bad. So this is not 'we do it in the morning; we do it in the evening' this is literally throughout your day that you pay such attention to it that, particularly going into transitions. You don't go into any transition until we've done some breathing and we've done some bending and some whatever. You can have great fun with this, or look on YouTube, there's millions of videos about stretching with children and breathing. This is throughout the day, particularly I would say, that hour before they start to go home. That's when a lot of the problems start because, although children might not know in their upper cognitive brain "oh I've got an hour to go" their (biological) systems learn the system.

Kathy Brodie: That's interesting. The internal clock starts to say "do you know what this this is going to be home time soon".

Jane Evans:. So, you know like some people have dogs and they say "Oh, my dog knows, my dog's at the window before my partner comes home - half an hour before, they're on the back of the chair by the window". And we hold memories in our bodies, more than we do in our brains. This again is a common theme. Early Years people will tell me "you know that hour or so before they go home" is difficult and by the time the parent comes it's really bad, and the reconnection is really bad. So again, we have a responsibility to pay attention to this and make that last hour one where we do some little hand massages. The older children we can teach to just rub their feet, rub their hands, rub the back of their heads. Then that transition back to the parent will be a much happier one.

Kathy Brodie: If you've got that calmness as well, things like hand-over chats about what's happened today, everything then falls into place. So what I'm hearing is that really this has got to be a whole setting thing. This isn't something as a one practitioner you can do. Does that come down from the leadership then of the setting?

Jane Evans: It really, really does. We need leaders who embrace this with every fibre in their being. Because the thing is that we have a complete crisis, definitely in the UK, and I know in America also, with children's mental health. In this country we don't have the services, our demand for mental health services for children outstrips availability by a massive amount. And it's not going to improve. And you know why. Because of these * holds up mobile phone *. So you know, what we've created now in our societies is, we've created a world that doesn't suit a developing child's body and brain.

Kathy Brodie: Oh how interesting. So is their connection with technology overtaking their connection their personal connection with people? And is that do you think that's what's underlying a lot of this?

Jane Evans: Yes it definitely is. If you listen to any of the world experts in childhood trauma they will they will cite screens as a really big issue. The optimum way that we came on to this planet, however we came, is to be in small nomadic tribes. So we stayed in our tribe when we were a child. We always had access to four caring, available adults. Now we say we're lucky to have two. And we usually have two who are on their phones to a lesser or greater extent because of pressure, pressure, pressure. Pressure from work, we are supposed to be answering emails even when we're not in work. Pressure from social media pressure everywhere, we're in the immediate world. So something pops on your phone you fight to leave it to the next day. That's like a big achievement. So all the children are growing up behind screens. And that that's against nature..

Kathy Brodie: Of course, almost by definition, the children that are attending settings or going to childminders are very often it is because Mum and Dad are out at work. Not always, but very often that's the case. So almost by definition, as practitioners, we are seeing those children who are exposed to that more than any other children as well. And that is in addition to us as practitioners undergoing those pressures as well. So they're just seeing it double, if we're not if we're not careful about that.

Those are some really interesting strategies. And to be honest that doesn't cost anything. That's just a change of attitude isn't it really.

Jane Evans: It really is. It's pretty much free. It's exciting to me. Just paying attention to it and having the courage to say - **this** is the priority because then the learning can happen. If you have a highly anxious child you rob them of their capacity for learning. You rob them of their capacity for curiosity. You can't learn if you're not curious. You rob them of the capacity of joy and you rob them of their capacity to be relational, be in relationships. These are really, really, really massive challenges for someone who's living their life like this * anxious face *. And that's lots and lots of children. But children need to have joy because, as we know as adults, joy is harder to find!

Kathy Brodie: What a fabulous gift to give the child - of joy! So that's something that's as practitioners we can do. Is there anything that policymakers can do is or any anything that we can lobby our governments to bring in to support that?

Jane Evans: Absolutely. In this country (UK) this week, we had the leader of the country, the Prime Minster Theresa May saying that she is going to prioritize mental health for children and young people. Yet in this country, and I know also in America, the focus is very squarely on academic achievement. But in reality what's happening is our children are getting sick because of pressure. So it's having the courage for policymakers to look at this very seriously and say "okay, we understand that until a child's emotional needs are met, until they're physically safe, their bodies feel safe, they can *not* learn properly and forcing them to makes them sick".

Kathy Brodie: Well in fact trying to force that learning on them, doesn't result in learning. It results in that short term regurgitation. And in fact there isn't any that deep level learning going on at all then is there?

Jane Evans: No, just lots of anxiety for them.

Kathy Brodie: I think it is absolutely high time that it should be given priority. In Early Years we've always said that personal, social and emotional development underpins everything. That's the foundation, you get that right, *then* they can start learning. We've always said that, but it is nice to hear some policymakers are at last keying into that as well. We are getting some rhetoric at least. So it'll be interesting to see how that varies around the world as well and how globally other countries are picking up on that.

So we've talked a little bit about that grounding and about practitioners having that as a whole setting. If you are just starting out on this journey could you give practitioners just one tip. One essential thing that they can do themselves tomorrow morning when they go into their setting to help reduce anxiety in their children.

Jane Evans: OK. learn to breathe into your belly. So if you watch a baby sleeping babies tend to sleep like this. If you watch them their stomachs rise all the time. Not their chests. So next time you're near a baby watch this, because that's nature's way. So when we have an open body like this it means we're relaxed, not frightened.

When we're like this * curled up * this signals to our body and our brain that there's danger and we're under threat. So it releases all the stress chemicals in our body. It gets us ready for fight or flight. So as we get older, we lose the ability to breathe into our stomachs - well, it's always there - but we forget to breathe into our stomachs.

So if I have a roomful of 100 professionals I'm speaking to and I say take a deep breath, what you'll see is * breathes in, rising chest *. Now that does not bring calmness to your body because you've just breathed into the upper part which is the bit that switches us on. "Da-da! Something's wrong".

The bit that is call 'Rest and digest' quite literally is below your diaphragm, so it's round your stomach, it's that part. When you breathe into that part of your body, it tells your body, which tells your brain, that you are safe. You are safe, life is good.

Hence why many children have stomach related problems, some bowel related problems and bladder problems because when we are very stressed. We live in our upper body. And have breathing problems and many others. But as a practitioner, if you again go on YouTube and Google belly breathing and it will show you. The best way to do it lie on your back and practice at home first because it's weirdly hard to do because we don't do it. It's literally breathing in through your nose and breathing down into your stomach, imagining you're filling a balloon as you breathe in. And then when you breathe out letting the balloon go down. It can be your Best Friend.

Kathy Brodie: That's a fantastic tip. I'm going to practice that!

Jane Evans: Honestly, I do it literally everyday, all day. It's the best thing you can do. With children, if you have a windmill and you blow a windmill or a feather they're trying to blow - that still introduces this idea of this long outbreath. You can have fun with.

Kathy Brodie: That's the sort of thing we'd be doing with the children anyway isn't it. Blowing bubbles all that sort of thing. That's a fantastic strategy. Thank you very much indeed.

I do know that you've got four Early Years books, but the one that deals with anxiety in children is 'Little Meerkats Big Panic'. Can you just tell me briefly what that's about, what sort of things does that cover.

Jane Evans: I talk a great deal about the brain and the body in terms of their relationship that they have and how amazingly we can help them settle us, particularly the body as I've been talking about today. It's the story of three animals - a meerkat, an elephant and a monkey. They actually represent the three main areas of our brain. So, they have a little adventure and they behave in the ways that those areas of our brain behave.

The meerkat is the survival brain that tends to panic all the time, the little elephant is very good at emotions and memories but not much else, which is our middle brain. And then the clever monkey is our top brain and it can work things out and it can make plans. And luckily, when things go wrong, they all find each other and the monkey, by helping the three animals do some breathing and have a cool drink of water, helps all the three parts of the brain reconnect and talk to each other.

Now, you don't get that explanation in the story, you just get the story of the animals. But at the end there's a simple explanation for the children about how this is our brain and we can help it feel calm in some activities. And then there's a slightly more advanced explanation for the adults of this being the three areas of the brain.

Kathy Brodie: That sounds fantastic. As you say that's a story you can share with the children.

Jane Evans: It's that simple. All my stories are very much aimed at kind of 2 to 6 year olds, although they're used by everybody of all ages but they're very simple, sweet little stories.

Kathy Brodie: And beautifully illustrated too, I have to say. They're published by Jessica Kingsley and there's a link to that on the website so you can click through to get those.

I know that you do training around the world and you speak about anxiety and trauma. Where can people find out more if they want to come and hear you or get you in for some training?

Jane Evans: Have a look on my website. By all means which is www.thejaneevans.com Email me. Janeevans61@hotmail.co.uk. Sometimes I put my own events as well. I'm kind of here there and everywhere.

Kathy Brodie: And of course you're a big Twitter person as well. And the link is Twitter is on the website: @janeparenting2 Jane, its been an absolute pleasure. I've learned so much. I'm going to lie down on the floor and have some very deep breaths in a good way. So thank you very, very much. It's been really thought provoking and I'm sure that everybody would be able to take away some of those strategies. Thank you so much for joining us today in the Early Years Web Summit.

Jane Evans: It's such a pleasure. Thank you very much for having me.

Kathy Brodie: And thank you very much to our viewers and listeners today for joining us today on the Early Years Web Summit about personal, social and emotional development.

CHAPTER 3

THE HIGH ACHIEVING, WHITE WORKING CLASS BOYS RESEARCH (HAWWC) PROJECT

Professor Chris Pascal OBE and Professor Tony Bertram

Kathy Brodie: I am beyond delighted to be joined by not one, but two professors on the Web Summit. We have Professor Chris Pascal OBE and Professor Tony Bertram. Anybody who has ever done any research in the UK, or has ever done a college course and referenced, will be very familiar with the (Pascal, Bertram) and (Bertram, Pascal) references. They're absolutely core to the research that we do in the UK.

They are also co-founders of the European Early Education Research Association. Tony is a past president and Chris is the current president. Tony also coordinates the European Early Childhood Research Association Journal. In addition, both Chris and Tony are directors of the Centre for Research in Early Childhood (CREC). They have both advised governments, in the UK and around the world, on early childhood issues. So I'm absolutely thrilled to be able to speak to them today on our Early Years Web Summit.

Chris Pascal: Thank you.

Kathy Brodie: The thing I wanted to focus on today on the Summit is all about personal, social and emotional development and the piece of research that you've done that really caught my eye was about High Achieving White Working Class boys, which has the acronym HAWWC (pronounced 'hawk'), which had some really, really interesting findings. And I thought we could just pick one or two of those findings and see where that takes us in our practice. So, before we actually start that, could you give me just a brief background of how you came to be researching this particular area please?

Chris Pascal: Well, it's an area or a group of children, White Working Class boys in particular that Tony and I have been talking about and dialoguing about for a long time for a number of reasons.

We know from the big statistical studies that they are probably the group of children who achieve less well as a large group, and so a lot of the issues around closing the gap and diminishing the difference, whatever you want to call that, but basically giving these boys a life opportunities to succeed. These boys are a big part of that community.

The other thing is that we both come, Tony and I, from white working class backgrounds and grew up in poverty ourselves - or what would be perceived as poverty with complex families - and so our own autobiography often speaks out in your research interests. Seeing that, in a sense, statistically how *we've* achieved, despite the odds, is something we've often talked about. That sort of resilience and what enabled us to do that. So we have the opportunity to, at last, to do a nice focus piece of research on how these young boys fared from their babyhood through to entry to statutory schooling to Key Stage One. And so that's where the project came about from.

Tony Bertram: When you look at underachievement, educational underachievement, which of course is different perhaps to underachievement in your life, but they are connected, when you look at underachievement educationally you see that there are three main factors.

To rank these: the first one that gets in the way of educational success is poverty, the second one is around, in terms certainly in the Early Years, around gendered issues. So boys develop later for whatever reason, predictably, and certainly in their language development so on. The third aspect is ethnicity. Ethnicity is often connected, certainly in England - and I'm not saying the U.K. I'm saying England - is related to aspiration and expectation. One of the factors that inhibits academic success is the fact that people say to themselves "in our community, on this estate, it's not for us". You've just got to get through the educational process and get a real job and work. So, when you look at these factors the predictive factors for underachievement educationally are first of all poverty. Secondly that you're a boy. And the third aspect is that you're white.

So thinking typically, there are large estates around our country where actually large groups of these boys aren't successful - that's what the statistics say. But we turned that on its head and say the statistics don't actually identify individual children. What we're interested in is - what about the boys who, despite those predictive factors, are actually hugely successful? Successful at the level that they are in the top 10 per cent **nationally** in the country. So that's your high achieving bit. We focussed on high achieving white working class boys to turn those stereotypical labelling aspect into something that was positive. What are the factors that enable these kids to fly? Thus HWWC = Hawk

Kathy Brodie: That's one of the things that really caught my eye. It's very positive research and that is very optimistic, as well in a lot of its findings. I think the image of a hawk in allowing a working class white boys to fly is just amazing - I think that's a lovely image.

Tony Bertram: For those of you who are old enough, you can refer it back to Kes, you know that's the story from the North East, the film about a boy who was clearly bright and intelligent, but the school didn't respond to it, to his interests and encouraging him to learn.

Chris Pascal: The other positive bit, in my mind-set and I hope CREC's mind-set, is an optimistic one. In difficult times you have to be. Seeing all children, and particularly this group, as full of potential and competence. Going in knowing that there is bags of potential there, that we that we have to work for and with.

The other thing is in our own research, the way we do research, which is very practice based, we think the knowledge resides in the communities themselves. It's not a group of experts from the outside who have the answers and then we tell the community what they should do. We wanted the community to develop or support community talking to community.

The idea, research wise, was that we'd identify this group of really high achieving, extraordinary achievement - in the top 10 per cent in the country, and let them tell their own stories. So, the idea is that we identified 30 or 40 of these high flying children. A group from Birmingham, a group from Oxfordshire - so city states, as Tony talked about, and rural poor in Oxfordshire; Northeast coastal towns in Scarborough and we had another group in the steel and shipbuilding area up in the Northeast in Middlesborough. And we identified these children and their families and they gave us the gift of their life, their stories.

We just asked them to tell us how they lived their lives from babyhood through to school age: what daily life was like; what they did; what as parents what did they do; as children what did they like doing. We talked to their practitioners, if they had been in a setting, not all had, but if they had we talk to these practitioners about these children. From those narratives, you'll see on the website, that we filmed them, many of them agreed to share their narratives through case studies and some of them talking to camera.

It's very much giving them the space to tell their own narrative their own story, to share their knowledge, not for us to construct the knowledge, because we think it's already there. What we did was provide a vehicle for that so community could talk to community in an empowering and affirmative and respectful kind a way. And in a way that said actually this is the optimistic thing – you're doing it! Many of you were doing this! But here's how we did this. And if we share that it might help you and that's true for the practitioners. There's a lot of knowledge there for other parents and the other powerful thing is that we learned a lot about these young boys too.

Tony Bertram: So this was at six (years old), looking back retrospectively at their life histories of up to then. What have been the factors that influence them and allowed them to fly in this way and be so successful at age 6? And I think we were a little wary at the beginning that we would find was kind of, to use a stereotype, distressed gentlefolks. So it might be that they were really middle class parents of these kids who had separated, so something had happened and that would be one explanation of why these kids, bright kids, were in this group. And then we thought or maybe it's just about the Tiger Mother idea, that there is someone there pushing them on and Mom pushing them on in that kind of aggressive way, that's been written about.

I have to say that neither of those stereotypes turned out to be the case. When we looked at this, it was much, much more subtle what was going on.

Chris Pascal: And that's the interesting finding, actually that it challenged some of this. But there was were two core things right at the beginning that really shocked us. And the big message for us in the field and sector.

So the first thing was, when we identified these high achieving boys - and we did that using the Foundation Stage Profile, so they had to perform in the top 10 per cent. When we talked to the parents about their children, they were shocked that they'd been identified because they were used to being identified because they've got a label. So shocked because something wonderful was going on in their lives, they had no idea. They knew their child is doing okay in school but nobody said to them "are you aware of how extraordinary your child is?" This young boy is in the top 10 per cent *in the country*, not just in the school or local authority but in the whole country. They had no idea. Nobody had ever said to them.

Tony Bertram: "Well I knew he was brighter than his brother, but I didn't realise he was *this* bright".

Chris Pascal: So that's a message - they don't even know. The thing was, when we started to talk to them and say tell us about life at home, tell us what your day is like and what you do as a parent. They'd say:

"Well, nothing special."

"We don't do anything particular."

"We just do it."

"I don't know why you're talking to me really."

" I can't really think of anything."

And then we'd say, OK, just tell us about your day. What happens in the morning? The minute they started to talk, this wonderful stuff would come out. Nobody had ever said to them "You are a fantastic parent".

In a way, they weren't extraordinary parents. They were excellent parents - in extraordinary circumstances. So they were doing all the beautiful things that you want a parent to do. We'll come on to what those might be in a minute. And it wasn't as Tony said about the 'Tiger pushy-pushy', but they were brilliant at parenting. Some of these families, these boys and their families were in extremely adverse circumstances. A lot of chaos a lot of challenges. In the group there was drugs, criminality.

Tony Bertram: Jeremy Kyle.

Chris Pascal: Mental health problems the whole realm of it. So it wasn't that they were nice, cosy, tidy, untroubled families. But they were able to do this extraordinary job of parenting really well in these challenging circumstances. And that's the extraordinary thing - excellent parenting against very difficult and challenging circumstances and situations.

Tony Bertram: We have to be careful here, because we are using the word 'parent' and actually that that covers quite a few different kinds of people. But people taking on a parenting role, the main carer. So sometimes it would be the grandparents that were there. Sometimes, particularly in the seaside towns, what you often find is that families have fractured and reformed with other families. And in that reforming there might be older siblings. And one of those older siblings would take notice of this young boy. And sometimes it was relationships like that within the family. Sometimes it was an aunt or an uncle.

But there was always somebody who had become the key player giving time to the child to talk to them and to be responsive to the things that were in the child. A lot of the stimulation actually started in the child. And what was happening, it wasn't people were giving the child lots of stimulation themselves, but the child was engaging with this key person, who was then responsive and created opportunities and affordances for this child to explore the world in the way that they wanted to. Its a different idea than the stereotype of the Tiger mother that's pushing, pushing and pushing.

Chris Pascal: Or putting them in a setting that's going to push and push and push. The one thing we found, these were not vulnerable weak children. They were very strong children, coming back to social and emotional development, something, from early on, that parents or main carers identified. Something in that young boy had been brilliant at enabling somebody in their extended family group, and I use this phrase, "to fall in love" with them.

They had managed somehow, and all babies have this capacity, where you have somebody in your environment that responds in the way that Tony's just said, to have this form this special bond. It generally was the birth parents but not always but somebody there was there to go to extraordinary lengths for that child to be with that child and be that child's companion. And it was a two way street.

Then what happened, very interestingly, particularly those carers who were in fairly challenging circumstances, the boy became the reason why that carer distanced themselves from the chaos or protected the child. The child became the reason why they had to do that. I think that they're very complex these family relationships, which Feinstein's recent work has shown. Its the relationships within the family that determined this, but this child, this young boy, was a strong powerful pull or push. There was one of the parents on the video, she had a very severe mental health problems, post natal depression, she brought this young boy home, she put him on the kitchen table in a B&B and she said "What have I done? I have no idea. I cannot go through with this". And then she said the midwife - and this is where key professionals can make a difference - the midwife that came to see her said "just talk to him, just talk to him". She said she started talking to him and we never looked back.

Tony Bertram: He helped her out of it.

Chris Pascal: While she talked to him, he responded. And they did that. So his voice was very powerful in inveigling the attention of this significant other.

Tony Bertram: And just to say that in terms of Early Years practitioners, because we also talked to them, what has this child done, so we tracked back to going to childminder's and so on. So we tracked back to the history and had a conversation with these people, if we could find them.

The first thing to say is that they all remembered both the boy and the parent or carer at 4 or 5 years old. Based on the relationship not only with the child, but actually with the family as well. And not only did they know them, but the parent or the carer remembered them as well. They'd established personalised, strong relationship that was strong. The Key worker and the pair worked together responding to the child. In some instances, where the staff had changed, a younger sibling had been taken to the same setting and the parent had said "you know what, I don't want to leave my kid here because it's changed and it's not like that and I don't have the same relationship." So in a sense they were discriminating about what kind of place they wanted to leave their child. All the way through the system there had been this good relationship where they had both worked together to support the development of the child. And that is the first thing to say really, that look not just your relationship with the child but the relationship with the context in which the child is in, in terms of their family.

Chris Pascal: So that's the focus of this conversation, which we always say it is all about relationships. And relationships are about the social and emotional competence of those involved. And these young boys had, from the beginning have that capacity, which was affirmed and developed further by the adults around them, responding back to that and developing that. And they were helped by (where there was professional input), by the professionals responding in that kind of way. So relational stuff is really, really, really important. Then we come back to the kinds of stuff that the "parent" used to do with this young boy.

Tony Bertram: I think one of the first things to say is that all of these boys experienced quite large amounts of time outdoors. From early days. It wasn't that they were playing football, although some of them were, but it was just they were *out*.

Actually, it was the parent who was pram pushing them out. I remember one of the parents talking to us, was about walking down the promenade, with the child and she just used to go out because it actually was therapeutic for her to get out the house. And she said "as I walked down the promenade, I was cross and fed up but then people started smiling at me and I was cross at them smiling at me."

Then she realised they weren't smiling at her, they were smiling at the child because the child is engaging and it's outdoor and pushing. All of them had some experiences, whether they had a as a space to play in, outdoors, and it could be a public space it could be just walking along a promenade or a road whatever. But that was quite an important element they had to have this body space and being active.

Chris Pascal: So the physical world, the natural world, the blend of being able to be more physical because they will definitely have more freedoms when they're outside. They also had the stimulation and that external of the natural world and the people within it, formed a big part of their daily happenings in virtually every single case. So it wasn't that they were cooped up doing bookish stuff all the time.

Linked with that was, whether they were indoors or outdoors, was this main carer, enjoying their company, just enjoy spending time together. And they did stuff together. Whether that be building, playing with cars, running about, there was a lot of physical stuff. It was just spending time, being a companion and of course what went with that was a lot of talk, that conversation. So these aren't extraordinary things, we know about these things. But when we think about how do you boost achievement, and how you apply that to practice - what are the big messages? It's about building a strong relationship. It's about doing stuff together, being a companion not an instructor.

The other thing was they would generally all talk about "well we just noticed what he was interested in and then we'd go with that". So the boys would express their interest in playing football, building something or even books, if it was books. One had got fascinated with music. By the time we talked to him and he was six he was writing his own songs and performing. Another one it was the football, he was being identified for a contract with one of these clubs, aged six. That's been noticed by the parent and the parent had gone with it, not trying to pull them in a way they wanted to be.

Home routines were there, but they were flexible not rigid, so they get to have a kind of bed time routine and a kind of food routine but not rigid. They were quite normal in terms of technology and TV screens and that kind of stuff, not extraordinary at all.

Tony Bertram: I have to say that the whole movement in Early Years at the moment towards an outdoor play, outdoor activity and learning in the outdoors, I think, is reinforced by the study. We're seeing that that's something that we should encourage. And as Chris says it's not about sitting the kid down at a desk and insisting that they colour in templates or whatever. So I would say, yeah encourage your children to learn outside and to be active and participate.

The other thing is that Chris just touched on is around digital - what we call digital childhoods. I've got six grandchildren all under the age of six on their ipads all the time and I'm thinking "what...?" This was true of these kids as well. They all have access to these, it's modern childhood. But it was managed, it didn't dominate what they did but it was *part* of their childhood. I think you've got to accept that it was used, as Chris said, it was controlled. So in relation to digital childhood, I think, yeah you give them the opportunity and you look for discussions that you can have around that and interactions that you can have around that, but you don't let it totally dominate the children's lives.

Chris Pascal: Actually what they would say was "well, he does that, but actually he'd much prefer to be outside, to be doing this, so that's what we did" because it was always what did he wants. They weren't little Emperors. It was just this congruence of intention and day and they just enjoy each other and if that's what he wanted to do then that's what we did, because that's what we had a good time doing. It was being in the company of somebody who is going to be responsive to you and the boy himself was a very big part of that. It wasn't the parent, in a very generous way, saying I'm going to give him this time. The boy made it so enjoyable that they *wanted* to do that. Even though their circumstances made that quite difficult for them. In some cases they were in a low income or poverty families. Because the mother said "I have to get away because of my child", they'd taken themselves away, in a sense they were even more focussed on each other.

That's the other issue of why we want to follow this group of extraordinary boys through because I'm really interested to see what happens as they go through primary school. Because for these boys, and they were very socially adept, they were very good in their own peer group too. They were really good leaders of that community.

Tony Bertram: They weren't bookish introverts scholars (some of them enjoyed books) but actually, they were socially competent. And they knew how society works, both in terms of your relationships with other adults and the relationship with their peer group. By and large there are popular group amongst their peers.

Chris Pascal: So in order to progress in that social peer group, which all of us need to do that, there needs to be a little bit of separation from the parents, because that becomes more significant and needs to become more important as they get older. The thing that's fascinating or interesting us at the moment is what happens next? So these lovely things have been going on that we've talked about and some of the things we found out, well, they've shared with us - been generous enough to share that with us.

Tony Bertram: So there's loads of stuff on our website. There's other podcasts and there are worksheets and practitioners talking of things.

Chris Pascal: We have no idea what's going to happen with this group next. As they progress through primary school and the peer group becomes more successful and relationships between the carer, the teacher and the child shifts maybe a little bit. And also fundamentally the relationship between the boy and their main carer, key carer, what happens next?

What happens for the boys, I think the peer group will take over, but for the parent, who is the protective factor in this from the other stuff, who have they got now? Because often this boy was who they had. Where do they go and do they go back into that chaos, do they retain it?

The other thing we are developing this concept - so we've got this concept of these academically resilient young boys - but we're developing this concept of what we're calling 'parenting resilience'. Now the boys were making the parents good parents. They were a resilient factor in parenting. That relationship that daily, intimate, wonderful relationship has changed, where's the parenting resilience? What happens to the parent at that stage?. How does the school support the parents in that shifting relationship? The boys are going to go through adolescence, challenging things more.

I'm positive that some of these boys and their peers will navigate that well. I want to know how it happens, because I think that's got all kinds of knowledge there that we could benefit from in terms of pupil premium, the way primary schools work, with this group. That is the next bit of the study we'd really like to do, as well as developing this kind of work in other communities.

The other thing we've got in each of these communities is these parents we worked with and we talked about developing their capacity, especially their confidence, their self knowledge. They'd worked with us on this project and developed confidence, so confident they can talk to the video, some of them. But they've all said we'd like to, we'd be really happy to, work within the community. So trying to develop parenting capacity for other parents. As resources are diminishing seeing that in every community, there'll be a group of wonderful parents that might be willing to support other parents. Trying to develop that piece of work around how do we better use that capacity. To liberate the capacity of the community to support each other and not "I'm the expert. I'm going to tell you how to do it" just like "this is real life. These were my struggles" "I can be a buddy or a friend" and we're exploring new ways of parent's support I suppose – parents-to-parents or family-to-family support that I think is another interesting follow on.

Kathy Brodie: I think that split when boys get that bit older, they need to find their own independence, they need to find out who they are and that naturally will diverge. But at no point have you actually said "oh we need extra resources we need to buy this". This is all about what's already locked in to these parents, to this relationship that's already there. But what we need is that information to come out is to share that knowledge within those communities.

I just think that be so powerful rather than having somebody come from somewhere and say "I'm an expert at this. This is all you need to do. And then your child will be fine". But to actually have somebody say "well, you know what, all these things happened to me and we managed to get through it okay". And if it was "I popped him in a buggy and took him down the front" - how simple is that?

Chris Pascal: They're not complicated things here but it does depend, going back to where we started, on that relationship. And I think Early Years practitioners in the sector understanding that - how deeply important those relationships were for those parents because they needed support too in these situations, they were giving a lot to the child. Where they had accessed a good children's centre or a good nursery school or a good Early Years practitioner that was an additional bit of magic that came in. And for those who managed, they would say they were a lifesaver. They were vital. They enabled me to go on.

So, although there's a lot of capacity in these families and parents, it also affirms that the practitioners too can, and many do, perform a vital role. If you get that relationship right. That's not judgmental. That's not labelling. Its affirmative and (in the same way as the parents were running alongside their child being a companion to the child) that the practitioner becomes the companion in a deeply respectful affirming way, in a respectful but also kind of challenging when that needed to. That was a vital bit in many of these stories, in these narrative.

Tony Bertram: I think there have got to be more subtle ways of approaching this than coming up to somebody and saying "we've identified you part of the troubled families, but don't worry we've got a program that's going to correct it. As long as you do our step by step approach you know. And if you don't do the step by step approach then actually we've got ways of penalizing or even removing benefits".

Chris Pascal: It can be punitive and if we're not careful and disrespectful. And suppose what we're trying to model and advocate for is a more compassionate, more respectful and more companionable approach that appreciates everybody's capacity and believes that people have that ability, that capacity, with a bit of support – it's not NO resource but it's about how you use those resources.

Tony Bertram: And looking for things that are participatory but also recognize that there's power and voice in this and then you have to distribute some of the power to others and listen to their voices.

Kathy Brodie: I think the idea that 'you will fit into this perfect mould that I have created for you' - that's a problem. I think it would be fantastic if you could take funding to both follow the boys through, but also to follow the parents. I can see there would be massive benefits for community.

I can just see that if these boys do go down a different path then there would be a cost to it. So if we can stop that and I think we have a moral obligation anyway, without anything else to have that funding to follow through.

Chris Pascal: And its about what kind of a society we want to live in and create and that the ethics and morals and all of that, it is about community and strengthening communities, social cohesion.

Kathy Brodie: And I think if there's one top tip I could take away from that is - it as simple as a practitioner saying to a mum

"You're doing a fantastic job. Do you know how well he's doing?" I think that would just be fantastic. Maybe we just assume that they know? And I think as a parent myself it would be like - oh, that's so nice!

Tony Bertram: I used to go with my kids to parents evening you know, dread that they were going to say something and you'd sit there for hours then you get five minutes that they looked through the paperwork, and tell you "Oh, they seem to be doing all right" and "I'd think - so what was that?". I think you've got to work on the relationship, which is different but you have create the space to develop that relationship.

Chris Pascal: Don't assume they know. In our experience we didn't have ONE of our 40 odd that had ever been told.

Kathy Brodie: But they were in the top few per cent in the country - not just in the setting in that area - *in the country*. Nobody had thought to tell them!

Chris Pascal: If you imagine that was a child from another community with a different set of relationships, they would be being promoted around every way. Those parents would have known, whereas these parents, they had no idea and that says something about aspiration and expectation doesn't it?

Tony Bertram: So when we say in the top 10 per cent, we are not saying in just one area, we're saying across the piece. It wasn't that there were brilliant mathematicians.

Chris Pascal: It was in that good level of development across everything. Think of that potential, you think of that multiplied up across the country. You think of that potential. What fantastic things those young boys, I hope will achieve - and the ones that will come behind them and what they might achieve, if we can get things a bit more supportive for them, a bit more affirmative and recognize what they are. That's the bottom line.

Kathy Brodie: And I think at this time as you say currently in the world I think that's a very positive message to be putting out there. There are children who are doing, and families who are doing, really well under very difficult circumstances. But they are still doing really well and that should be celebrated, as well. I think that's a great message to put out there!

Now I know that you have a big conference coming up in this summer in Bologna.

Tony Bertram: European Early Childhood Educational Research Association conference in Bologna.

Kathy Brodie: And that's called 'Beyond the Crisis' and that again is looking at things in a very positive way looking at research where. It is similar to your research, where they have found very positive things. And that's from the 29th of August to the 1st of September 2017 and there's a link now on the website you can just click through to that and go and have a look and see.

Chris Pascal And Tony Bertram: Some fantastic speakers and a thousand researches from all over the world, focused on Early Years - is just going to be incredible.

Kathy Brodie: If you're a researcher in Early Years, that's where you need to be in the summer, it's just going to be incredible. And I shall look forward with interest to see what papers come up at that.

Thank you very, very much indeed. Absolutely amazing to talk to both of you. Thank you so much for organizing that between you really, really do appreciate that and there's some really interesting things there. I would urge everybody to go and have a look at the HWWC research. I was absolutely thrilled reading through it, all the positive messages that are coming out there. The simple things that people are doing and it's been excellent discussing it with you.

Thank you very much indeed Professor Tony Bertram and Professor Chris Pascal, really appreciate your time today.

Chris Pascal And Tony Bertram: Thank you. Kathy thank you. Thank you.

Kathy Brodie: Thank you very much to our viewers and listeners for joining us on the Early Years Web Summit.

CHAPTER 4

WHY ARE DROP OFFS AND PICK UPS SO IMPORTANT TO A CHILD'S DAY?

Dr Suzanne Zeedyk

Kathy Brodie: I'm absolutely thrilled to be joined by Dr. Suzanne Zeedyk, who is a research scientist fascinated by baby's inborn capacity to communicate. She has been based at the University of Dundee since 1993 within the school of psychology.

In 2011, she set up her own independent training enterprise to disseminate more widely the science of Early Years and spends much time speaking to the public about our human need for emotional and psychological connection.

She's able to bring this to her research expertise on topics including parenting, infant relationships, family support, communicative disorders and the sociopolitical context that frame our responses to scientific information.

She works closely with organizations throughout the world to increase awareness of the decisions we take about caring for our children, illuminating the way in which those decisions are intricately connected to our vision for the kind of society that we want to build today. Welcome to this summit Dr. Suzanne Zeedyk.

Suzanne Zeedyk: I am so delighted to be here. It's very visionary of you Kathy to offer this information to people so far across the world. I'm just delighted to be taking part.

Kathy Brodie: I'm thrilled that we can put it around the world. It's amazing isn't it? Today we're going to be investigating drop off and pick ups, as a particular area of personal, social and emotional development. But before that could you tell us a little bit about why you are so keen on spreading this message of connection please.

Suzanne Zeedyk: Absolutely. As a scientist I know that we have discovered all sorts of things about the importance of human relationships for our well-being and our basic functioning in the world. But I also came to realize, after 20 years producing scientific insights that an awful lot of people who worked with children (and indeed with adults) weren't aware of that information. So I got really interested and working to see how we could translate that science to the wider public.

So, that's what I did five years ago, was to step away from full time academic work in order to try to reach the public. That's a whole range of people, that's childcare and social workers and teachers and parents and politicians and manufacturers of baby buggies and retailers and musicians and police - anybody who is interested in understanding more about how human relationships work and how they affect us biologically. If we understood that, we would have a much better sense of how to solve many of the social problems that we face. And so I spend all my time now just trying to help make those scientific insights accessible for people and take away some of the big words that often scare people and help them to really apply theory and knowledge in real life settings. And I love it.

Kathy Brodie: Yes. That is quite a range of people that you're talking to there! As you say, that communication is human isn't it? it needs to be across all those areas doesn't it?

Suzanne Zeedyk: Well, it's when you get the basics of how important connection and relationships are you begin to realize how you know how widely spread it is. And the thing that's really important about the Early Years is that the brain is being shaped in some quite fundamental ways, during those Early Years in ways that we didn't know even 20 years ago. But what we now know about how brains develop and why experiences are so important, has often not yet reached parents and professionals. And it doesn't mean that the brain doesn't go on to develop in other ways later on. And it also doesn't mean that you can't heal from early difficulties, but it *does* mean that if we understood how very important the Early Years were, we could think better about the kinds of services we set up, we could think more deeply about the kind of care that we provide, and we could spend our money more wisely. So that's why one of the reasons that Early Years information is absolutely so important as well.

Kathy Brodie: From an Early Years background, I couldn't agree more! But particularly I'd like to look at the area of dropping off and picking up. So that's when we're dropping our children off at settings - and it doesn't matter whether that's a childminder or a daycare setting. Could you expand a little bit on why you think that such an important part of a child's day?

Suzanne Zeedyk: Absolutely. As I was thinking about this I thought actually there are three key reasons that drop off and pick up, but especially drop off if we just think there for a minute, are so crucial.

One is that they set a child up for the day because most often drop off is happening in the morning. For some children it is happening in the afternoon. So that's setting you up for the rest of the day. But the way in which drop off happens sets you up for that day. It has a biological impact. Often we think of it as just behaviour, because that's what we see. But that's the point of all this connection stuff is that our experiences in the world, and especially of other people, especially as children have a biological impact on us. It's going to produce changes in children's hormones in their body. It's going to create connections in their brain about what partings are like. It's going to have a biological impact and that's going to set you up for what comes later because of your biological state.

Secondly, it really is going to shape your brain, especially if you're young, because your brain is developing more rapidly between birth and three (and even a bit before birth) than it ever will again. So children's brains are learning what the world is like and they're building connections and little neural connections as a result of those experiences including drop off. We all know that drop offs are very difficult for many children and we can come back to why that is.

But then thirdly the reason that drop offs are important is that because of those lessons that the brain learns, it sets up what partings are like for the rest of your life.

Kathy Brodie: Wow that's pretty powerful.

Suzanne Zeedyk: It's very powerful and it becomes really important to today's world because so many of our children are now in professional care. In the past many children will have been in the care also of grandparents or other family members and lots of children still are. But somehow we don't think of those as partings in the same way. And actually we probably don't handle them in the same way.

Kathy Brodie: No that's true we don't.

Suzanne Zeedyk: So thinking about the way in which professional settings and professional care - and our adult thoughts about what professional care should look like - shapes children's unconscious experiences about what partings are like. That is going to go on to shape your biological expectations, that are unconscious, in your marriage and your friendships, in your partings from your parents, when you fly in on planes in future. All of those partings and re-unions are being shaped in these very Early Years and our children now have them every day, many of them, when you are in professional care. So I think we need to think about that a whole lot more because it hasn't received nearly as much certainly scientific attention as it should. And a lot of practitioners are just winging it without special guidance. So I think that we should think about that.

Kathy Brodie: I know that you think about drop offs and pickups as that classic attachment moments don't you? So I know a little bit about attachment, but if you could just tell us a bit more about attachment and how that relates to drop off and pick up please.

Suzanne Zeedyk: Sure. It's such a great question because it totally knits together the real life with the science.

Attachment is basic. There are lots of ways to describe it. It's basically our craving for relationships in our lives. So human beings have a biological need for connection to other people. And we live in societies that are more and more disconnected. So that's one way in which we need to think about the importance of that biological need. All human beings, whatever their age, have an attachment system and a need for connection. What happens in the Early Years, because our brains are developing so rapidly and we're learning what the world is like, is that we unconsciously learn what relationships feel like and whether they feel emotionally safe or they feel a bit anxious. All of that is unconscious and we just come to think of it as normal as we get older, because we don't have a lot of conscious memories often of what is happening in those really Early Years.

So one way in which we're learning how relationships function is when we part from other people and when we have reunions with them. In fact, when you think about that, it becomes fascinating to realize that all cultures have greeting and goodbye rituals. Of course you do that in different ways. You have a handshake or you give people a hug or you give them a kiss or you give them three kisses on either cheek or you rub noses. Or you have a word that says hello or good morning or good afternoon or good evening. I love thinking about that little tiny thing because we just do that without ever thinking about it. But there they are reunion rituals.

And that's even to people that were there the night before. So all the people in your house you still say "Good Morning" to. And I can make people laugh by saying, you roll over if you're sleeping next to somebody in bed and say "Good morning, darling" (or you scowl!). I'm not supposed to say that because you know that seems a bit intimate, but actually it's true.

Then we go to wake our children up and - think about this - and this is where suddenly everybody who's listening to this will now be going "Oh my gosh, yes, I shout at her or I play soft music" or I say "Get up you're late for school again" - and you will, they are all rituals. How you say Good Morning and Hello.

We also have parting rituals. So we say goodbye or shake hands again. And if you say goodbye and then you realize you've forgotten your umbrella. You have to come back for it, somehow feels embarrassing because you've already said goodbye - those are attachment moments.

Kathy Brodie: I always think about attachment as being with babies and young children, but you're absolutely right, I've never really considered as adults we are still replaying all those things that we learned. When I say goodbye to my mum on the phone, I do it exactly the way that she's always told me when I was a child so we're repeating those rituals as well aren't we?

Suzanne Zeedyk: That's just the way we develop. That's the way relationships develop. They start early on and with children they start early in development and then it just feels normal.

Once we get that idea of normal and thought about unconscious, we can then start to think about - what if normal actually is uncomfortable? So normal can feel safe or it can feel anxious. It can feel easy or it can feel uncomfortable. If you're a child with this rapidly developing brain those feelings become part of the whole phenomenon.

If we link that then to the science, attachment research has been going on since the 1940s and it picked up a lot in the 70s. One of the key researchers was a woman named Mary Ainsworth and she developed a procedure called the Strange Situation paradigm. Nobody who's listening to this has to remember any of those. But it's helpful to think "Gosh, there's a procedure, a scientific test that looked at partings and reunions".

What the scientists did, and it still used, is that you bring a mother or father into a setting, in an unusual setting, an unknown setting. And then after you've been there together for a little bit the parent goes out of the room, leaving the child in the room with a stranger. And then the parent comes back in about three minutes later. And the key things that you're looking at in that is how the child copes with the parting and how the child responds to the reunion. And also how the adult participates in all of that.

So that parting and that reunion is what our children do every day when they get dropped off with someone else. That someone else could be a group setting, it could be a childminder, it could be a grandmother, it could be a grandfather, it could be your neighbour and its still a parting.

We think of it as a parting at the beginning of the day and a reunion at the end of the day, but actually it's both, both times because you part from your carer and you have a reunion with your professional care. So you part from your mom and you have a reunion with your childminder, for instance. At the end of the day you part from your childminder and you have a reunion with your mom. Then, that becomes interesting, because we think of it as a kind of a parting at the beginning of the day and a pick up at the end of the day. Actually it's both.

Now is when it gets really interesting to think about what does that whole transition feel like for a child. Well, let's take a really stereotypical one. Mom brings the child into a group setting, into nursery and already the child is feeling anxious. And actually if we roll back in time, maybe the child has been getting anxious the whole time she's in the car. So the anxiety is already building, because she knows she's about to get dropped off and she doesn't want to. In fact, mom's getting anxious because she knows this parting every day results in tears. So now already they're anxious and I can make this really worse. The child's in the backseat in a car seat, so the only way they have to connect is through the mother's voice. If the mother is feeling anxious that that will show up in her voice even if mom's trying really hard to hide it. The child's very attuned brain can hear that.

So now we get there, we're already anxious. We get to this setting - and I'm calling it a setting, so we can think about those professional words. A child doesn't think of it as a setting. You know, it's kind of interesting to think what word would a child use. Now they might use the word nursery because that's the word that they've been given. But really for them it's another home, for them it's part of their life. They don't know that the people there get paid to take care of them. And their brain thinks that they're part of their family that's what children's brains are meant to do.

So they really think that it's Auntie Kathy or Auntie Suzanne or even if they call them Mrs. Smith. Their brain thinks that's part of their family, their clan, their tribe. Well what happens if that person who they really come to like, because it's their auntie, isn't there, because nursery thinks it's a service. And so they just have a random person who receives that child. Or maybe they're not a random person. They're one of their one of 10 people. But that means that that child never knows who's going to be there to welcome them, to help them part from their mother or their father or their granny or whoever is dropping them off. And so maybe that's part of the anxiety for the child is that they never know what is going to happen, who is going to greet them. And if they're struggling and that person isn't able to help them with that struggle, so you drop them off and let's say some settings think that you're not really allowed to cuddle children.

There's been interesting discussions, in 2013 and 2014, there was quite a lot of discussion in the media about whether settings should be able to cuddle children or not. That's why it becomes important to think about the way adults think about it. If we think that this is professional and that professional means that we're not meant to cuddle children - in fact we're not meant to cuddle them because we're slightly anxious about touching children, which many professional settings are. When you cuddle children it helps them to feel safe. It helps them to calm down. It helps the hormone called oxytocin to rise in their bodies. And that helps them cope with the disappointment and emotional pain. And so if we're not cuddling children in the middle of this transition, we're not giving them the biological help that they need to cope with something that's difficult for them.

So several things in that long account I've just given you there, are that the way we think about this as adults, do we think that this is professional - and that means we need to be distant - will shape it. The staff rota, will shape it because it's your staff rota that that makes it possible for the key person to be present for that child. Also, if you have a start time where a number of children arrive all at once, and many settings do, many group settings do, you don't have time to pay attention to individual children because you've got lots of children all around which is different for say, a childminder.

And so once we start to think about these tiny details and realize that they're crucially important for a babies and a young child's brain, we start to realize that drop off at childminders is likely to be very different from drop off in a group setting. Those lessons get built into a child's brain and they unconsciously carry them into the future and now they're going to be dropped off at school in a few years time. They've had very different drop off experiences, probably, if you've been dropped off at Granny's as opposed to dropped off at a childminders, as opposed to dropped off at a group setting. And we just don't realise and we just call it 'drop off'.

Kathy Brodie: Exactly. And that's very often what schools say "have they been to a setting before?". Very rarely do they say was it a childminder, was it a grandparent, was it a large group setting, a small group setting - they just ask have they been somewhere else and, as you say, that experience is going to be vastly different isn't it?

Suzanne Zeedyk: Vastly different and we have no research that tracks that over time. So children who are struggling in school... Just imagine that you have a child who's had a long history of drop offs that were uncomfortable. And now it goes on to be dropped off at school. As soon as they're starting primary one, they're starting in a different emotional place about separation from parents, than children who had more supportive experiences of drop off. So if you start your day with cortisol in your system, that's a stress hormone, that if you had difficult drop offs you would have more of, you're starting your educational day with a higher amount of stress hormone. That impacts on your ability to learn.

Kathy Brodie: That's it's a biological, hormonal level. And what we're doing is actually flooding children's bodies with that hormone by the way that we handle those things.

Suzanne Zeedyk: We are. Now, having said that, there are lots of things we can do to help. Here's what my brain is doing right this moment. I'm now thinking about all the people watching this. OK. And many of them may be professionals. So they're thinking about their professional practice. But many of them will also be parents. So when I talk about attachment connection I'm trying to help it to be really real and not theoretical but I walk a very difficult line because as soon as it becomes too real, lots of us go into a place of guilt. "Oh my gosh, I didn't know that when I was dropping my child off. I just did what the provider suggested. I knew she was crying but I didn't know how to help".

So right now there'll be a whole lot of people listening to this that are feeling guilty and I don't want anybody to feel guilty. And yet I want us to take this information seriously. So the challenge is: how do we hear this information, that feels anxious for many of us because we want to do the best for our children that we can. How do I get us to take it seriously and yet not tip over into feeling bad about ourselves? The answer is that we do the best we can. We work with the knowledge that we had at the time. No child needs perfect parents and no child needs a perfect childcare provider either. Relationships are not perfect they are messy. That's attachment.

The crucial thing to realize is that there may have been consequences left over from earlier in life that could help explain what we are struggling with now. Understanding that gives us a way to tackle challenges that we might have now. So if you suddenly, looking back over your life, realize I could have had really high cortisol levels there, then it's likely that you still have high cortisol levels at parting. So you can start to pay attention to what you struggle with.

So, for instance if you do attachment theory, and some people watching this may have heard of avoidant attachment patterns or a ambivalent attachment patterns (if you don't know about those it doesn't matter, but just to say there's a fancy name for it). People with ambivalent attachment patterns struggle in distance. They struggle with partings. So their body starts to go "Oh the person I love hasn't told me recently that they love me and they still matter to me". So I start to get kind of unconsciously anxious. Lots of people out there who identify with this - you send a text and you don't get a text back. So you send another text, you start to get anxious that you're not going to text back. I try to make it funny but the thing there are people who identify with it. The lack of getting a text back starts to raise cortisol levels. People go "that is really silly. Calm down". But if you have been wired to be anxious about partings in a sense that the cortisol levels are rising.

Kathy Brodie: That's almost your 'go to' place, that's your default setting as it were.

Suzanne Zeedyk: Yes. So if you can then start to be aware in adulthood, or teenagehood, that is where I get anxious, I get anxious in the parting. You can start to think about what is going on biologically and then you can start to go "OK. How could I help myself with that?" So yoga and meditation and all these bodily practices, help breathing when you send your text and you don't got a reply.

But other people are more anxious on the reunion and that's one way to describe avoidant attachment. If you are into all that disorganised attachment, which often comes from extreme trauma, is anxious at both distance and closeness. Imagine how difficult that must be!

Securely attached people are pretty OK with both.

I've gone way up to grownuphood there, because it helps us to get it, but if I come back to what we're supposed to be talking about here, which is drop off pick up, we can now see how your child's experiences of drop off and pick up are about reunions and partings and why they are so important. In our modern western world, we have children in professional care in a way that we wouldn't have had in evolutionary history of human beings.

Kathy Brodie: And we've got that double whammy going on at the moment, haven't we, with more and more children going into settings. Also that attachment theory is a relatively new kind of theory, certainly, the 70s is when it gained most popularity wasn't it? So that's a reasonably new area as well. So we've got both of those things coming together there but I've never thought about how that impacts on further life...

Suzanne Zeedyk: Well Kathy, if I can interrupt you for a second there. I think it's fascinating to think about the fact that we have had attachment theory since the 1970s. A whole lot of people don't know about it and therefore can't make use of it. So, actually in some ways at one level I think it's kind of shocking that we could have had Mary Ainsworth doing her research, which is about partings and reunions, and we have not applied that to drop offs and pickups for childcare. So part of me says that is not new. That has been around a long time.

In fact that goes all the way back to the 1940s and 50s with hospital practice. So, very briefly, in the 1950s children who went into hospital were parted from their parents and didn't see them for days. And so now we think that probably created some emotional difficulties for many adults in the world but they didn't know yet. OK. So that's a whole other conversation is hospitals.

But here's another thing to think about attachment theory. Many people know about attachment parenting. And that is now a huge debate. So you read all over the papers at the moment - Should we be using attachment parenting? Does attachment parenting make parents feel more guilty, when you have to be parted? Does attachment theory make women especially feel guilty? Attachment theory as we know it in the wider public has not helped us often to feel calmer. It has often made us feel more anxious. And I don't want it to do that because I think it has hugely helpful things to tell us about the biological functioning that we all do as human beings.

If we can understand that it's about the way in which it influences our biology and how that taps in now to a lot of the study of trauma, we can see its value in new ways. And so that's what I'm trying to help us to do - step out a lot of the anxiety and help us to step into curiosity.

Kathy Brodie: Yes. And you said right at the very beginning that often we're dealing with the behaviours rather than the actual core root of what was going on. That is the hormonal changes and so on. So very often what we're doing is just putting a sticking plaster on those behaviours at the end rather than going right back and saying this is where it's come from. This is the core root of it.

Suzanne Zeedyk: Totally, because we see it as behaviour. Somehow we have this cultural message that says 'I as a parent (or childcare staff) my job is to deal with behaviour'. But if we begin to get the message that all behaviour is driven by an emotional state, an emotional need and that emotions are biological, we can then get curious about behaviour.

So I was reading a piece about temper tantrums and how tantrums are about a child's often need to discharge a lot of emotional energy. And how we are embarrassed by it because children kick and scream and shout. And if we're in public you get embarrassed by the behaviour. Somehow we think that it's about us as parents managing our children's behaviour. You can go on courses for managing behaviour.

Well I would use the language of responding to emotional needs. And if we see all behaviour as a request for emotional help, then we begin to read all of that behaviour differently.

Kathy Brodie: Oh absolutely. It's a much more positive way of looking at it as well. Rather than saying tackling behaviour and challenging behaviour - it's quite negative isn't it. But 'meeting emotional needs'. Who wouldn't want that? You know I just think that's so powerful.

Suzanne Zeedyk: If we begin just by changing our language it gives us new insights. I can think of a school that I have worked with in Fife who just changed their language from 'challenging' behaviour to 'distressed' behaviour and they say that it transformed their school.

Now I know we're talking about drop off and pick up but because that taps into attachment, all of this helps us to think about attachment needs in a much bigger way. And that school was able to really meet the needs of their children and they were able to do that a much better way. Not because they got in a big emotional management program, but simply because the language that they were using, changed the way they were reading children's behaviour. So that's a really inspirational message for lots of schools. And is just as applicable to child care settings as it is educational setting.

Kathy Brodie: I just think that's fascinating that I know a little bit about attachment but making all those connections - I don't think I've ever kind of made them all the way through to our adulthood. So what sort of research is there that's going on at the moment in this sort of area?

Suzanne Zeedyk: There is very little research going on about drop off and pick up. I think that's because it's just so normal. It's just a normal part of every day. We often miss the scientific insights and value of everyday experiences. I don't know why. Because if what we are learning about children's behaviour and the way brains develop and the importance of relationships isn't relevant to every day - then why are we getting that information?

So there are a few papers that have looked systematically at drop off and pick up but there are very few. So if there are scientists or there are students watching this perhaps that's a little flag. You're saying that would make great projects.

Kathy Brodie: It would be a fantastic Masters dissertation wouldn't it, would be amazing.

Suzanne Zeedyk: So what that leaves people doing, since we don't have a whole lot of evidence to draw on, is one of two things.

They either might make the link from theory and that's what I'm doing here. So when I'm talking about the importance of drop off and pick up it's because I can't cite a whole lot of studies that have systematically studied drop off and pick up, which is often what we think of as evidence. Instead what I'm working from is our theoretical knowledge about the importance of brain development and the processes involved in that, about what we know about attachment, and I'm applying all of that really valuable important theory to a specific situation of drop off and pick up. And some people have wondered if that is ahead of the data.

Well, if attachment tells us about the importance of relationships and drop off and pick up I think it's a perfectly legitimate and helpful application. Once you understand how the process works you don't have to have applied it to every single tiny situation in order to gain insights.

In fact, that general theory helps us to think about the reunion and parting when you're putting a child in a car seat or when you're lifting them out of a car seat and getting them into a high chair and when you're taking them out of high chair or when you need to go to the loo and you're going to leave them in the front room for just a minute. Those are partings and reunions as well, they're just tinier ones. Now we have no research that is called "What to you do when you are going to the loo".

But we have attachment research and brain development research which would still be very helpful in thinking about those moments.

Kathy Brodie: Sometimes it is bringing together all those different disciplines and all those different areas where the insights come. It's not until you put all those layers together that you can see the whole picture forming is it.

Suzanne Zeedyk: Absolutely.

Kathy Brodie: I know that in England we certainly have the requirement that we have a key person system and that's based very much on the attachment theory and the idea that you have that connection and I know there's a lot of countries, they call them different things, but they do have special people that you drop off and pick up from. But are there any guidelines or anything that governments that you know of about drop offs and pickups?

Suzanne Zeedyk: That's a brilliant transition into thinking - OK where are people getting their ideas about how to do drop off. Because we do them every day. When you start to think about OK so where do we get our ideas about how that should happen?

And it's happening in one of two ways. Either you are applying this theory, best you know how, or you do it intuitively. Most people are doing it intuitively, which makes total sense, because we do goodbye's and hello's intuitively all the time, so why wouldn't you do drop off and pick up at professional settings intuitively as well? But everybody who is engaged in that knows how awful it can get. It can be very stressful, it can be very stressful.

In fact I had a mother who e-mailed me just this morning

before we sat down to do this, who said she'd been to hear a talk I'd given and I'd mentioned drop offs and pickups and she was writing to ask could I help. Because they talk a lot about it and she feels really confident in her relationship with her daughter but she still says we say goodbye and she is inconsolable. So she's thinking a lot about it. And this is a childminder. So it's one on one. And she's still saying that her daughter is 'inconsolable'. So this is what she's asking "how can I get more teddy bear moments to overcome this sabre-toothed tiger moments of saying goodbye?"

And I'm reading that, so that we can think - there is a real mother out there today who needs to hear this and would find this helpful. But she's also using this language, that I use, of sabre-toothed tigers and teddy bears to give us a different way to think about this.

So internal teddy bears for me are our capacity to comfort ourselves. When I get that text back and I get anxious, can I comfort myself? Because the sabre-toothed tiger moment is the parting. Or for some children the sabre-toothed tiger moment is the reunion. And then for some couples the sabre-toothed tiger moment is reunion, in other words sabre-toothed tiger is a moment of fear.

So you ask where do we get guidelines and really what should we be doing? That's why the language is so important. How do I help this child comfort themselves in the middle of what is a stressful moment? So the word comfort makes me think as an adult I have to help this child comfort themselves. And if I can do that, they will be able to comfort themselves in the future.

If I'm not helping them grow an internal teddy bear, every single morning and every single afternoon when you get picked up, I am not building their resilience. Since I am, as an adult, participating in this, if I don't think that partings are a very big deal, because they don't bother me, I might not understand why this child is inconsolable. So I might not be very attentive and attuned because they don't bother me.

All of this requires us to get really curious about what that behaviour means for someone else. And to get really curious about where their sabre-toothed tiger moments come and why that is such a struggle for a child and how I can help to support them and grow a stronger internal teddy bear, to use my language.

Kathy Brodie: I think that's a very powerful image as well because the sabre-toothed tiger in the sort of fear - fight or flight and all sort of basic emotions that start to come to the fore then. And that's exactly the sort of behaviour that you see.

Suzanne Zeedyk: So then that leads us immediately into OK what should I do? And this is when we can start to think about what guidelines are out there because some child care settings do have guidelines, but many of them don't, because we have not thought about this.

So if we just take a basic attachment thinking like we've been talking about, here are some things that tells us:

Never disappear! A standard way of doing this in the past, but not so much anymore, was that childcare staff, understandably because you had the sobbing child (and they're not all sobbing). I've described a lot of sobbing children and I suddenly think I want to stress this is not anxious for all families and all children. So they're not all sobbing and for some of them once they were sobbing. But they're not anymore.

But I don't want to take that for granted because then it lets us think, what happened for that child that it is not so distressing? What happened in that transition? Or actually they're not crying but they're stuffing anxiety so you don't necessarily have to be crying for it to mean anxiety. But the behaviour that we tend to tune into most is inconsolable crying. So the advice used to be "just go, just go. I've got them just go and he'll be fine later". But here's what a child learns if you disappear without having said goodbye: A child learns that a parent can disappear and they don't know when that's going to happen.

Kathy Brodie: That's what you're teaching them isn't it.

Suzanne Zeedyk: Yeah that's exactly what you're teaching them without ever having meant to. We teach our children lessons, we didn't mean to.

So, the first place you have to get curious and forgive yourself, if you think I taught them that lesson because you're doing your best.

If you learn that your parent can just disappear, that's not a comfortable message to learn. And so being able to say goodbye and participate in that is really important and most child care settings now, when you talk to them, that's what they do. They're not saying - just go, but if they are childcare settings out there who are still doing that now I'm hoping that this conversation will help them to think about that in in new ways.

But it also means that if a child is sobbing a lot that you need a key person who can help them while they have to do this difficult thing of say goodbye to mommy or daddy or granny. Then what they're learning is that, if I have to do this hard thing there is someone to help me. And in best practice they would be there to help me until I feel really recovered. But I have sat in settings and 'really recovered' can takes till lunchtime.

Kathy Brodie: Yes. And of course he might be being picked up soon after lunch as well so you're starting that cycle all over again.

Suzanne Zeedyk: If you have a staff ratio that doesn't permit you to sit with a child on your knee until lunch time, what do you do? And the question we need to ask ourselves is - what do we do? Because if we just go - well I can't provide that - we need to understand we are shaping children's attachment patterns. I know that it causes us some real difficulties, but we need to engage in that.

There are nurseries trying to take this on board who have changed their staff rotas. Some of them have their staff work longer days. So a four days a week, but for longer days. Some of them have considered the financial implications of changing staff rotas.

We need to hear from more nurseries that are really trying to take on board the importance of drop off and pick up as attachment moments to hear how they're handling that.

Kathy Brodie: Do you think there is much awareness out there of how important this is?

Suzanne Zeedyk: No! So when we start to understand the basics of attachment, and in this case drop off and pick up, we can then start to think through the practical implications and perhaps financial implications and the staff rota implications.

Staff are supporting both the children and the parents, so some settings now call parents to say here is how they're doing. Because if you see the parent off to work and they're anxious about this difficult parting that we just had, they're having trouble focusing on work because their cortisol levels are high.

We call it 'childcare'. We don't call it 'parent care' or 'family care'. Actually child care settings are family care services. Which is why I really like playing with language. So if you call yourself a 'family care service' what does that mean we are responsible for doing?

So drop offs and pickups are these crucial transitions during the day. As a childcare provider you are responsible for facilitating that. Even if you didn't know it until you just heard that. Because parents do, largely, what a child care setting has them do.

So let's jump to pick up because we haven't talked a lot about that. Here's what happens in a lot of child care settings, because we're trying to do the best we can in a environment that now says we need to report on how the child's day was and we need to show you the things we wrote down.

In many settings a parent can walk through the door, you have a child over here who's been waiting all day long to see mommy or daddy and we greet you at the door. We say "Hello Mrs. Johnson or Mr. Johnson. let me tell you how she did today. We had a great day. Now she fell over. We had to put a plaster on her knee and she didn't really like the grapes at lunch."

Now the whole time your child is still running around over here. They are so anxious to get back in your arms. But what is happening is that you are having a conversation of information.

In an attachment led reunion you'd flip that. So the priority would be facilitating the reunion of the parent and child, in a way that feels good for that parent. And *then* you would do the information exchange.

Kathy Brodie: That's a really simple strategy that makes sense. That really makes sense.

Suzanne Zeedyk: And once you get attachment theory it's obvious which is why to go back to our earlier point - we've had this since the 1970s. How have we not used it to help us think about this?

I hope that anybody who's listening to this will go "oh I can do that". Here's the problem. Or here's **A** problem. If a parent is listening to this and they want to try that in their child care setting, but the child care setting doesn't know about this, the parent will have to be very brave. They will have to say "No. I want to change the system and I want to reconnect with my child first". So it's possible that the system won't like that or that the child care provider could feel offended or anxious. So it takes a very brave parent who might know about this, but wants to do something different from the child care setting, if they're not sure if that's OK with the child care setting.

So it's really powerful to have child care providers know about this; think about this; know that they are setting up the rhythm that will help their parents to step into and feel safe about. Now, if they can also provide some attachment information that explains why they're doing that, then that typically makes everybody really excited.

Kathy Brodie: As you say the theory is there isn't it is? There to be used.

Suzanne Zeedyk: Here's another tip that applies here. Turn off mobile phones! Because in today's world it's now very common, more and more of us are addicted to our phones and we hear about how phones are interfering with relationships.

What attachment theory tells us is that when I reconnect with a person who I've been missing, what I need for a split second or longer is their attention. On average hugs last three seconds, of course, that will vary by culture and things. So you think three seconds doesn't sound very long. But those three seconds are cut off if I'm looking at my mobile phone. My child comes running out of school and my parent is just finishing that task of sending on the mobile phone. And then they tune in. But that moment is lost. And so it's really important to be very present as an adult in that moment before you make a reconnection.

I was meeting a colleague at the train station a couple of weeks ago, who I was very excited about seeing but her train was late, so I was doing things on the phone and all of a sudden I thought "Suzanne. I think that you should apply what you talk about. You don't know when that train is coming in, but put down the phone so that when she walks through that barrier I'm present. Yes. And my face is saying welcome." It's really simple but it's not easy, if we become addicted to phones.

Kathy Brodie: But again, a very simple strategy that it's so easy to do isn't it. And again settings can talk to parents in settings. "We appreciate you're very busy but could you just put your phone in your pocket before you even come into the car park". And then you know that they're going to be there and present ready for the children.

Suzanne Zeedyk: Because we now know that's shaping their brains. That's going to make their marriage better. People laugh because you know "Their marriage better? They are two years old!"

Attachment teaches us that's what you're learning, this is what relationships feel like. And then, if I really push this Kathy, at the cutting edge of science that many people don't yet know about is that we can even map dementia symptoms onto attachment patterns.

Kathy Brodie: That's really interesting. I will put a link on the website.

Suzanne Zeedyk: So all I'm trying to say is that this extends across the whole of the lifespan in ways that we haven't thought about. And we're doing an Early Years Summit and most of the people I talked to are Early Years. I and others could help care home with the elderly but they don't get this kind of information because that's not in our general awareness. So I'm just really trying to help us to see how important these little tiny moments are.

If I say one more thing. So, we just talked about a few ideas about drop off and pick up. In today's world more and more children are not dropped off in settings by their parents. What happens is children get dropped off at a childminder. The childminder drops off at nursery. The drop off happens when they get picked up, they're picked up by the child minder and then their parent picks them up from the childminder. So if you think about that that child has had one, two drop offs in the morning and reunions and one, two reunions and drop offs in the evening - they've already had four major experiences of parting. And every single one of those are important, whether they're our child or they're a child we're caring for and we just need to think much more about that as a society.

Kathy Brodie: Yes and I think you're absolutely right it's cultural as well isn't it and how that society takes that as a norm is a given. This is what happens, almost without thinking of those consequences. And so we've looked at a couple of top tips and a couple of really easy strategies to employ there.

But, excitingly, I think you've been creating some resources to help communicate that real importance to drop off and pick up. Are you able to tell us a bit more about those resources at this point?

Suzanne Zeedyk: I hope that the training films that we've been making will finally be launched. We've been trying to get these out for months now. But of course there's only so much time and I have this little tiny team that we create these with. So if I just had three lifetimes we'd have all sorts of resources.

In terms of drop off and pick up we have been creating films where we literally filmed drop off and pickups in nurseries and then narrate those to help people see in detail what's happening for children. What we try to do show is really positive drop offs because this helps us to think again what kind of resources do we need.

Very often the drop offs and pickups where children are struggling the most are the ones that are most informative for us as viewers but they don't feel good for people who did the drop off even if they didn't know. So it becomes interesting to think about how could we see that what could we create. Do we need animations? Would that be helpful? It just helps us to think more broadly but what we've been doing is putting together films of positive drop offs and then narrating it and slowing them down so you can see what's happening.

We also have at the moment e-courses that talk about wider attachment and within those I talk a bit about drop off and pickup and hormones in bodies and brains. So they're e-courses that we have at the moment. We have a suite of three courses actually.

We have books which are meant to be short and accessible on attachment but also some of the other topics within this. In fact one that we have is on dementia. So that was already out there and we have some others that are due out shortly.

We have a whole raft of videos and handouts, information sheets on my web site. And we also now have little teddy bears, which are little teddy bears which I mean not just for children but also for adults. I often think of them as sitting on the top of your computer, because computers are a place that can cause frustration, and they have little T-shirts on them with "fighting sabre-toothed tigers" on them because Teddy Bears are what help us fight sabre-toothed tigers. They're meant to help us laugh but to be a reminder that all the time I need to be drawing on my internal teddy bear and I need to be boosting his or her capacities if I think they are struggling in some way.

So we have tried to come up with all sorts of resources that are just fun reminders or training or mind is for people. But in terms of drop off and pick up we have these new films about to come out.

Kathy Brodie: There's links on the Web site to that so people can click through. And just to remind people that your web site is www.suzannezeedyk.com if you search and that is the first one that comes up and I know you're a big Twitterer because I follow you obsessively. It's @suzannezeedyk again. And Facebook. Tell me about the stuff that you do on Facebook, that's really exciting.

Suzanne Zeedyk: Well on Facebook I put up a post every night about connection and disconnection. And so it's there for anybody who wants to follow it. You know some weeks when we reach about 50,000 people, just people sharing and I do that because they're often news articles or they might be new research reports or their videos you know just on YouTube. So they're just ways of helping people to take their science and apply it in real life. And I purposely post a whole wide range of topics so that we keep in mind how widely this really applies. So every single night there's a new post there and it makes it easy for people to share.

Kathy Brodie: So I just think that's amazing. I can imagine that, because it's so wide, that there will be people in the staff room saying "Did you see that one? Can we discuss this in the staff meeting" because this is going to be something that for everyone, it's just amazing. So that is really good.

Suzanne Zeedyk: I still can't believe how well social media works and in spreading the word because sometimes I'll put out a post and I get up in the morning and it's been shared and it's reached 30,000 people and you just think how did that happen overnight?

The other thing I should add Kathy is that you can also search under Connected Baby. So Connected Baby is what we produce all the resources under. So it gives us more of an organization because I want these ideas to outlive me. And so Suzanne Zeedyk gives you often my particular take on things and Connected Baby is where we are creating the resources that more people can draw on because I didn't want it to be you know the Suzanne Zeedyk theory, because it's not. It's about connection. And so when we started producing resources I wanted a name that really captured that we were about connection and about the importance of those baby years even if we are talking about adult life. So both of those you could search under.

Kathy Brodie: Thank you so much for joining us today Dr. Susanne's Zeedyk, it's just been amazing. There's so much I'm going to have to go away and look up as well and just remind myself all those things. But that has been very, very interesting. Thank you very much indeed for sharing all your expertise on the Early Years Web Summit with us today.

Suzanne Zeedyk: Kathy thank you so much for having me. I've been really honoured and it's been great.

CHAPTER 5

SUPPORTING THE PSED OF CHILDREN AGED BIRTH TO THREE

Julia Manning-Morton

Kathy Brodie: I'm very excited to be joined by Julia Manning Morton. Julia's career in the early childhood field has included roles as a practitioner, advisor and inspector across a range of settings for children aged nought to seven.

A senior lecturer in early childhood studies for much of her career, Julia's particular interest and passion has been to support the development of children aged birth to three, being part of the Birth to Three Project Group. Her research writings focus on PSED and she's particularly interested in working with teams and leaders to meet the emotional needs of babies and young children. Welcome to the Early Years Web Summit, Julia.

Julia Manning Morton: Thank you Kathy.

Kathy Brodie: I'm absolutely thrilled that I've managed to get the guru for birth to three. I just think it's going to be fantastic. Today we are going to focus on personal, social and emotional development, as I said that is one of your key areas of interest. So we're going to look at children age from birth onwards, so take it right back to those very beginnings. What is it that is particular about personal, social and emotional development and babies?

Julia Manning Morton: Well can I just say first off what a huge area this is and how we are very used to saying 'PSED' very quickly and it being one area of learning in the English curriculum. But, of course, it's three areas and it's massive in term of ideas and thinking and practice. So I think we have to be very careful. I mean we're not going to be able to squeeze everything in, but it's also very difficult in practice to squeeze it into one area of planning for example. So I think that that needs to be thought about.

The other thing is that it's a continuum. For me, social, emotional and personal development is lifelong. And here's the thing. Even now as adults we continue to learn about ourselves. We continue to learn about other people and social ways of doing things. It's important for us to keep that in mind.

However, having said that, the foundations, those very important building blocks, begin from the very beginning - if not before birth but certainly from birth and those foundations can give children either a very positive start in life or a more challenging start in life. I think that is why, for me, this area of learning and development is hugely important and that it's hugely important that we get it as right as we can for our babies, toddlers and two year olds.

When we think about the personal, social and emotional development of our youngest children, I think the key issue that we think about primarily is their physical and emotional dependency. It underpins this aspect of development. This dependency means that they experience their emotions, for example, really, really intensely and express them very, very clearly through crying screaming, whatever it might be. Now this is really important because if they didn't do so their survival might be endangered. This is an evolutionary skill that human beings have developed and is very necessary. Physical dependency also means that babies and very young children experience their emotions very physically. And the physiological aspects of feelings are very strong. The feelings of hunger, coldness, discomfort, are really, really important and can cause huge amounts of distress for very young children. But, although they might communicate that very powerfully and let us know in no uncertain terms that there's something wrong, their distress is often very generalized. It depends on the skill and intuition, the attunement of the adult to know what is wrong or to try and work out what is wrong. A toddler who has a shoe that is rubbing and causing them discomfort is really whingy and it might be really not obvious what the problem is. It's the adult's responsibility to actually think about what might be the issue and get right underneath that and work it out. So this requires caring adults, practitioners and parents to know these children very, very well.

The other reason that the emotions of babies and very young children are expressed very immediately and without any kind of mediation is because of the development of their brains; at a very, very early age emotions are being processed primarily through an older part of our brain, the limbic system, which is the part of our brain processes our emergency emotions, so when we perceive a threat of some kind and we go into fight or flight mode. Everyone will experience that - road rage is the classic example.

The expression of those emotions is not mediated by the prefrontal cortex of our 'thinking brain' and the connections in that part of the brain don't start to be made until about six months. They reach the fullest density at about two and a half, which might help to explain how much emotionality is going on in that age and those connections, those neural pathways, are actually not completely firmed up and fully developed until early adulthood. That's why one of the reasons I say this is a very long term development. It's when those connections are made in the prefrontal cortex that those inner feelings start to become understood and also gradually start to be able to be managed and regulated. But how that happens, of course, depends on the experiences of a young child and how their feelings and emotions are understood, accepted, mediated by the caring adults.

Clearly, as you know, children grow older and become more autonomous and independent and their cognitive understanding grows, both their abilities and their verbal and language communication skills grow, their ability to express their emotions and to therefore regulate those emotions becomes more sophisticated.

One of the things I'd like to emphasize about this is that being able to manage your feelings is not that you either have it OR you don't have it. It's situational. You 'lose it' sometimes, however mature you think you are. Given enough stress, fear, enough anxiety we can lose control of our emotions. I think we have to remember that as adults, just to try and help us remember that we experience that - even when we are in control of most of our lives. Babies, toddlers and two year old are not in control of what happens to them and their experiences, so I think we can understand how those kinds of emotional collapses can happen more frequently for them.

Kathy Brodie: Yes. And the suddenness, of course, with which they come on when you're flooded with those emotions all of a sudden.

Julia Manning-Morton: We'll come on to thinking about more about kind of the stress that young children experience. But if you if you can remember that young children experience stress sometimes from what might seem to us quite ordinary situation like going to the doctors or being in a noisy supermarket. This gives you sensory overload, which, when you're very young your senses are much more acute than when you're older. So you are taking in more and your ability to filter out sensory information is much less so you are being bombarded with sensory information and that can lead to overload and a meltdown.

Kathy Brodie: So we start wired up with the flight or fight as you say that's for survival and evolutionary purposes and then gradually as babies grow into toddlers there have all these emotions, all the outside sort of the world is now impinging on them and they've got to deal with this somehow some have and you've already touched on that. It's got to be sensitive practitioners and parents that understand and really know their children. But what are the implications if we don't? What happens if personal social emotional development is neglected during that critical sort of first few years?

Julia Manning Morton: I think there's a lot of research that shows that certainly the first three years and some neuroscientists will perhaps suggest the first six years of life, are particularly sensitive for learning about yourself, other people, your feelings and how to regulate them. Young children learn about these things in their close relationships with adults and central to this is the close attachment relationship that they make with primary carers or those very few close members of their family in the first instance, then, possibly later their key person in their early years setting.

Now, the optimum experience for a young child is one in which that close carer enables them to make an attachment with them through their sensitive, responsive interactions. It's those nurturing interactions and that means being what Daniel Siegel called 'being attuned' and you may call it to be tuned in. That attunement is whereby the adult aligns their state of mind with the state of mind of the child and mirrors it back. So you have a hungry crying baby and you are gently holding - you physically hold and you mentally hold and this also relates Wilfred Bion's theory of 'container contained' - these are psychodynamic theories.

So we hold the child in our minds and we take in their feelings and we say "It's OK, we know you're hungry but your food is coming soon. I'm just doing the bottle and you'll have it soon". We use a very soothing tone of voice and we use gentle touch. Through that, the baby starts to experience that this distress, this really frightening distress, is being managed by somebody else and that somebody else gives it back to them in a manageable way. So the child absorbs this idea that yes this feels horrible at the moment but I hear this soothing and I feel this soothing. And then I actually intake the soothing through the breast or the bottle and the child learns from that, that the distress doesn't last for ever and gradually becomes able to manage their distress and so on. It's a model of how that works.

Now, that is an attuned adult, who takes on and takes in the child's feelings. That of course doesn't always happen. Children can have psychologically unhealthy interactions with their key adults as well. Mis-attuned interactions with adults who are self-absorbed and concerned about their own issues: Adults who through depression perhaps, aren't able to take in the child's feelings.

So in those kinds of situations, the baby or young child doesn't get their feelings acknowledged. Those kinds of interactions can lead to insecure attachment relationships. The child would still feel attached to their carer but they will be learning in that relationship that they can't expect anything much from someone else. Those children either become very 'Only I can look after myself, I don't need anybody else'. That's an avoidance attachment relationship. Or perhaps they cling even more and just can't let go because 'if you go I won't know what's going to happen'.

So one of the things we know is that children who have chronic and repeated experiences like that - and I have to emphasize this is this repeated experience, it's not someone having an off day - every parent has an off day - or several. But generally the child has responsive interaction with those adults.

Those children, who have generally a secure trusting, relationship can get over it. Its just a blip and they might get stressed but they come down from the stress. It's children who have repeated, neglectful perhaps abusive relationships, their brains are always in fight or flight mode. Levels (of cortisol in the brain) are so high, so they're always on red alert or a lot on red alert.

Their levels of anxiety and stress mean that their learning is impaired. We all know we can't think when we're stressed. The ability to think is really impaired in this situation. Of course, we know that there are very negative outcomes for a lot of those children: Their later learning in terms of their ability to have positive relationships with other people etc.

However, having said that it's not a good/bad, all or nothing situation. There are plenty of us walking around leading (and I include myself in this) generally positive lives, generally successful lives in all kinds of ways, who may have an element of an insecure attachment patterns in the way we think about relationships.

The research seems to show that there are some children who, despite a very poor early start and those negative relationships, do seem to manage to make some kind of success of their own lives and their relationships. I'm not talking about earning lots of money. I'm talking about being able to feel okay about yourself, positive relationships. Now the research seems to show that those children somewhere in their lives, hopefully in their earliest lives, have had an adult who has believed in them and supported them and given them that positive feedback. They have offered them, if you like, an alternative model to a relationship than the one that they learned in their families. Bowlby talks about a mental model, a blueprint, in our minds of relationships and that is the blueprint that children take in to their future relationships with other people. What we have to remember in our practice of course, is that children come into our settings with a model in their minds of how relationships work already. Where children have had negative models, they will expect that from you as a practitioner, they will try and recreate that relationship.

One of the huge skills of the childhood practitioner is to be able to recognize and offer an alternative model of relating and relationships to our youngest children, so that they can perhaps say "oh right, it doesn't have to be like this", "Actually when I make a mistake I don't always get shouted at". "It is not quite as devastating to make a mistake, so therefore perhaps I can take a few chances in my learning".

So that's what we call resilience. So resilience doesn't mean being hardened and not caring. But resiliency is being able to bounce back from mistakes and to have a generally positive kind of view of challenges and being able to get over them, being able to get over a setback.

I think this is really important for early childhood practitioners to understand because they have the opportunity to offer children who have a very negative model of relationship to offer more positive or alternative model which hopefully will give children the resilience to survive what otherwise might be very difficult early experiences.

Kathy Brodie: I think that 'bounce back ability' as you say is vital. It's a vital life skill that not just for the birth to three is it? That's throughout life.

Julia Manning Morton: Absolutely.

Kathy Brodie: So that's really interesting, the idea that, as practitioners, we can give children those models. We can demonstrate that, we can obviously model that for them, we can support them. When things do go wrong, as you say, that they are allowed to make mistakes and not be penalized for that. What are the sorts of strategies and what are the sorts of things can practitioners can be doing to support the very youngest children in our settings?

Julia Manning Morton: Well first of all, the issue of

attunement needs to be understood by practitioners. Attunement is where you are tuning in, basically, but not just to what you see on the outside, but to what you understand to be going on emotionally, internally to your children and you hold that for the child.

So, you take it in for the child and you process it and give it back to the child in a way that is manageable for the child. So we talk to children don't we, we say "oh my goodness, you know, you really must be uncomfortable in that poopy nappy. Let me let's go take it off and make your nice and comfortable again and then we can play". You take the distress and the discomfort and you translate it into something that's manageable for the child; in that way the child will held by you physically, but also mentally. They feel held in mind and we do that with children all the time. So that attunement is very, very important.

Kathy Brodie: So I think that's slightly different to what I would call 'tuning in'. Tuning in for me is very much understanding what the child's interests might be, knowing the context. But as you say 'attunement' is then putting that into something manageable and handing it back and saying "it's okay I've got it here". It's almost got an element of empathy in there as well hasn't it.

Julia Manning Morton: Oh it's totally about empathy. Technically it is 'affect attunement', so it is that emotional tuning in. And so it's about taking in the child's feelings and holding them. This is called containment. So holding them and then giving them back to the child in a more manageable way, in a way that the child can think about them. By you thinking about the child's feelings you're helping the child to think about their feelings and therefore process them and make them manageable.

Kathy Brodie: Yes so that sort of idea of rather than a two year old having a temper tantrum this is a distressed child. And when you kind of think if I was distressed I wouldn't want to be saying "Oh, you're just having a tantrum."

Julia Manning Morton: Exactly. I call them emotional collapses. When everything just gets too much and my brain can't even process this anymore. So I have to fall on the floor. That physical collapse that goes with the emotional collapse is really really... It gives us the message, it seems like everything's gone, all of my ability to hold my body even. Sometimes it might be a learned behaviour to get what you want. But to condemn a child for that, to blame a child, that is not helpful. Maybe if the child has learned that way - quite an extreme way - of trying to get their own way then you know, how sad is that?

Most emotional collapses are not just about getting what you want. Most emotional collapses are about overload and not being able to hack it anymore and just falling apart. It's sometimes called fragmentation of the self. We 'lose it'. We talk about losing it totally and actually what we're losing is ourselves, so children are losing their self, their sense of cohesiveness.

Kathy Brodie: Well if you translate that into an adult situation you can suddenly see why that's such a major event for a child and just to say "get up off the floor, you're okay." That's really not helpful then is it? So attunement is so, so important. Having empathy and holding the children in mind which I just love. I love that visual image of just that containment and holding of children.

I'm thinking particularly about practitioners that are working in the baby room that are working with babies all the time maybe or childminder's who maybe have one or more babies in their care, what would your top tip be for those people who are working with those babies or with those very young children?

Julia Manning Morton: Oh my goodness. Let's think about

this. I think my top tip would be to learn as much as you can about why and how these children grow and develop and behave as they do because knowledge is strength. The more you understand, the more you're able to process for yourself those issues through your mind. If you're processing those issues through your mind, you're also being the container, the holder of the child's ability to process those things through their mind. So that's key.

But to be able to do that you need an environment in which you can think stuff through. You need, hopefully, someone you can talk to about what's happening, in a supportive and knowledgeable way. Proper support and supervision for practitioners who work in groups is really key. And for childminder's some kind of forum where they can share their thoughts and feelings is really, really helpful if possible.

Kathy Brodie: So let's explore working in teams a little bit further because my feeling is that sometimes practitioners in the baby room do feel a little bit isolated, or maybe if you're childminder and you're working with very young babies but maybe none of your colleagues are. How can team working support children's personal, social emotional development?

Julia Manning Morton: Okay. That's such a huge question because what we're talking about here is the psychodynamic theory of containment - container contained - and that's what the adult mind does for the child - holds the child in mind. You process their distress, their excitement, their interest, their 'self' through your mind and you give it back to them in manageable ways: "Oh you are hungry aren't you? Let's get your bottle straight away." "Oh wow you're really excited by that. I can see that because ..." We process that for children and we give it back to them in a manageable way.

Practitioners almost need the same kind of thing they need a forum or a place where they can think their practice through. They can say "I'm exhausted. I've had three babies crying all morning". And they need somebody to really hold that for them and talk them through it not saying "Oh what's the matter with you?". You know, "can't you hack it?".

Opportunities for reflection and support and supervision is key for practitioners working with all children, but particularly for those working with our youngest children, if they are really going to be able to free up their emotional minds to the children. Because what happens is that because the stress of working with very young children builds up and up and if it has no containing, no support, and no outlet, then what practitioners do is cut off to preserve yourself. You can't keep taking in all this because it's a very highly emotional process.

(If) you don't have a forum in which you can think about that, process some of that, then it gets too much and you tend to start shutting it off. As a practitioner you can stop noticing what's going on for children. You can stop responding as well as you might think. Because it's too much - your emotional jug is up here.

I often use this image of a jug. In it is coming all this stuff from the children and we are giving out. Well, actually you know we're giving out from our jug all the time - to our children, our parents, our colleagues. What we need is positive stuff that goes into that jug to refill it. How do you keep it well stocked? and the emotional jug needs to be well stocked.

And so practitioners do need opportunities to really think about what's going on, what's really going on with the toddlers. How are they managing to respond or what's difficult, how they're managing in that triangular relationship that is so important with parents and children? It's a triangular relationship and the sides of the triangle need to be equally considered.

Kathy Brodie: When you talk about supervision and forums, we're not talking about formally going in and sitting with the manager and having written down the sign here and that'll go in the folder. I'm thinking that you're talking about something much more emotionally supportive and being able to just off load sometimes and say "you know what, it's been awful this morning. I don't think I've been there as much as I could have been". Just to have that emotional unload is it. Am I right there?

Julia Manning Morton: It certainly isn't appraisal. It's certainly not about just ticking boxes or have you done this, that or the other.

Equally it's not just sitting and moaning. It's not just offloading; something constructive has to come out of that. And so it's about exploring what is going on and why you think it might be going on. And therefore what you might do about it. The process of that is helpful in itself. But there is also a practical pragmatic aspect of it because it needs to give you something to go back into your practice. It's not just about just offloading or a moaning shop. It's about thinking very creatively and concretely about what you can do in a similar scenario as well. It's fundamental really, to what I call an emotionally intelligent practice. If you're going to be a key person and let's agree (we haven't even talked about it!), I think that the key person approach is obviously fundamental to any kind of positive practice happening with our youngest children

If you're going to be a key person and you're going to be able to respond in an emotionally accessible and open and thoughtful way to young children and you need a forum where you can explore those interpersonal and intrapersonal dynamics of your practice with somebody who is knowledgeable, understands and can support you in that. That cycle can bring you round you into being able to respond positively and provide well for the children.

Having those opportunities for practitioners who work with

very young children is really, really important. That means developing in teams, it means developing a vision of practice that incorporates those emotional dimensions. That acknowledges that reflecting on those issues is important and that you're not somehow 'less than' or not such a good practitioner because you open up about finding something difficult.

Kathy Brodie: I think it's very interesting when you do university courses as yourself teach your own courses as well. And you sometimes find that that sharing community on the course happens as well - you see the practitioners sharing and discussing those ideas. And of course for some of them it'll be the first time they've come across reflective diaries and formally reflective rather than just having a think on the way home, they're formally reflecting on their practice.

Julia Manning Morton: Absolutely. But what's key about that is that there is some kind of structure to it, perhaps a more experienced other who can hold or contain the thinking and feeling to move it on to something that's useful. You know just a moaning shop isn't useful. It just goes round and round and round and round. It needs to be processed in a way that's going to be helpful and to go back into practice. This is our aim; it's making the experiences of our babies, toddlers and two year olds really positive. That is what is key. If we accept that our youngest children need positive relationships, positive experiences of close relationships in their early lives because from that comes their positive sense of who they are and their positive abilities to relate to others and understand others.

For me this is fundamental. You can be well developed in another area maybe cognitively or in terms of something or other. But for me real success in life - and I'm kind of quoting Daniel Goleman here - is emotional intelligence. You know, real success in life is about being able to know yourself, understand yourself and being able to understand others and hold down mostly positive relationships with other people. It's what makes the world go round and if you have those skills, then the other skills, the cognitive skills, linguistic skills etc. hopefully come a little bit more easily.

Kathy Brodie: That's a really nice positive message to end on there. Julia I know that you're currently running in the key times level 4 Certificate in development practice provision and that is specifically for birth to 3 year olds and that's with Early Education. I was very excited to find out that you're actually writing a book on personal, social emotional development for Early Education. So I'm really, really excited about that. I'll be looking out for that. I already used your two year old book loads, that's on my shelf upstairs already. But the Level 4 is part of a suite of courses. And you do level seven in birth to three. I got that right.

Julia Manning Morton: The level seven is not totally focussed on birth three, it's mainly focussed on PSED but with very much an emphasis on the very earliest years because so much important happened in this area at that time.

Kathy Brodie: That's really exciting. So if there are people working out there with babies who want to find out more who want to take their development that bit further, I just think that would be a great thing to jump on too.

Julia Manning Morton: And of course that's on my Web site.

Kathy Brodie: And that's on your website which is www.key-times.co.uk. And I know you'll be doing the Hackney conference as usual in your local area. And there's Saturday morning ones for childminder's there as well. So if you are in that area and you're a childminder do get yourself down to the Hackney conference which is about emotional well-being this year so that's a nice little link there. I'm so pleased that you agreed to join us today because your birth to three doesn't get enough coverage to come to the expert, has just been amazing, so thank you so much for that this much.

Julia Manning Morton: Yes. Well it's actually this much of THIS much.

Kathy Brodie: I like to think of it as an aperitif. It's just that appetizing idea for people to go and find out more about - it's really, really important absolutely vital.

Kathy Brodie: Thank you so much Julia Manning Morton for joining us today on the Early Years web summit.

Julia Manning Morton: Thank you very much.

CHAPTER 6

A MALE PRACTITIONER IN A FEMALE ENVIRONMENT

Rob Fox

Kathy Brodie: I'm really excited to be joined by Rob Fox today. Rob has worked in schools from London to Italy, although is currently based in Cambridge, working as a team member at the Stephen Perce Foundation where they care for children from age three to 18 and are innovative in their philosophy and their ideas towards educating children.

Rob feels sharing good practice and networking with others helps raise the bar for everyone and I really agree with that. In addition, he would also like to see the male/female barrier broken down in the Early Years sector for the benefit of the children that we care for and educate. Rob is currently studying for his foundation degree at Chelsea in Kensington College in London. A very warm welcome to The Early Years Web Summit, Rob Fox.

Rob Fox: Hello Kathy.

Kathy Brodie: I'm really excited to talk to you as a male practitioner, somebody starting out in his career as well. And I particularly wanted to look at attachment and how that fits with a male perspective. But before we start on that I thought we'd get a little bit of background. How did you start in the Early Years sector yourself?

Rob Fox: It seems to be a bit of a long journey now. It started off about six or seven years ago where I did some voluntary work in a local school and it was coming back with glitter on me and paint and my mum said to me "You look like you're enjoying yourself". And I said I'm never going to make any money. She says is it the job satisfaction or is it the money element that's important to you? That led me on to doing a level 2 course. It was the summer. I was - do I do business or do I do Early education? I did a level two course in college.

Then I did the two year level three program at Cambridge regional. It gave me an insight into a range of different settings. And it kind of enabled me that I had the strong interests of working with young children.

Kathy Brodie: So you kind of picked up on that I feel for being with children.

Rob Fox: Absolutely. So I did a two year program at Cambridge Regional College. After that I worked in day nurseries in Essex and in Herfordshire for a period of time. I really wanted to teach. I wanted to work within an education setting. But I couldn't get a break working within the school so that's where my journey led me to Italy. And then I managed to get my position as a transition teacher. A short period of time before returning to London and then going on to Cambridge with my current role now.

Kathy Brodie: So did you find that in Italy it was very different to what you'd already been used to, that you'd been working with?

Rob Fox: I taught on the International Baccalaureate for a period of six months. It was an eye opening experience. But in terms of the way we worked with the Early Years Foundation Stage and the way the IB works, there are some similarities. But having trained be an early educator in the UK it kind of brought me back to wanting to be back at home. Its what I'm passionate about doing.

Kathy Brodie: Did you find you have any challenges as a male practitioner?

Rob Fox: I was welcomed with open arms, completely, in terms of they're very family orientated individuals. They welcomed me with open arms. I didn't have any problems.

Kathy Brodie: Well that's really good to hear actually isn't it. I'm very pleased to hear that you are now studying your foundation degree. You obviously will have covered attachment on that. We're looking at personal, social emotional development, so I just wanted to have an exploration of what you felt attachment was as a male practitioner, because I know when I've when I've done the Men in Childcare that very often they'll say, well it's the parents who don't want the children to go to the man, or they might have issues so I thought we'd just get your perspective on that. What do you think about attachment as a male practitioner?

Rob Fox: Well I have to say I've not experienced any imbalance or anything. And I think it's down to the settings. I've worked with and a close network. I've always had another male there to be of reassurance to me and as a role model. Growing up, I had a male mentor whose mum owned a small day nursery in Hendon, Essex. And even from that moment on, he role modelled for me. The relationships build the trust you build with parents. I was able to see what he did, and what I did was kind of mirror that.

I think it's in terms of male attachment and building those relationships day in, day out and building that trust and enabling parents to see you as a professional within the industry. We can be seen as glorified child carers rather than educators and enabling those relationships to flourish that enable us to say "Actually I am a educator, I am a carer and I am a professional". I obviously demonstrate you need male traits, whether this can be recognised in me as a male, so I don't see there's any kind of bias.

I try and look at the individual child for who they are and each individual parent. It's a case by case and recognising what their needs are and what their interests are, in enabling them to feel safe and secure whilst you've got them in your care.

Kathy Brodie: Yes of course and that's security and feeling safe is an absolute bedrock isn't it, for starting on those attachment and relationships.

Rob Fox: Absolutely. There is also understanding, and demonstrating the understanding, of children's emotional intelligence as well and having prior knowledge of the individual stages of development. This helps me support these children that I care for and educate. Understanding insecure attachments and also just being culturally aware of the different attitudes within society, enable you to work better with each of the individuals that you work with on a daily basis.

Kathy Brodie: Yeah I think that that cultural aspect is quite important is it understand the community that you're working in as well and seeing that the bigger picture is it.

Rob Fox: Absolutely.

Kathy Brodie: Now I know you've got a Facebook page and I know there are discussions going on there. Could you tell us a bit about that please.

Rob Fox: I set up 'Recognizing the Unique Child and Educator in Practice' as a hosting service to communicate different challenges, different ideas that are happening within practice. Often we are lost within our own environments. We all work very long hours (some more than others). And it's an opportunity to network any concerns, any training ideas, any ideas that work within your setting, to truly make sure we're all singing off the same hymn sheet.

Kathy Brodie: As you say that's a really valuable things have on a Facebook page because we all do work different hours and be able have an afternoon off to do some reflection just isn't possible is it.

Rob Fox: No absolutely not.

Kathy Brodie: But I think those Facebook discussions really do throw out some really interesting ideas. It does get that dialogue going doesn't it?

Rob Fox: Absolutely. And it's been interesting to network with different professionals across the world and to say "I am having this challenge. Has anybody else had this challenge?" Actually often within our profession, we think we're the only ones with that problem. And as much as we talk to a colleague or a friend within the setting, sometimes it's better to have those conversations with people outside on a confidential basis who you can say and share ideas with.

Kathy Brodie: Yes. Because as you say those settings can become very isolated can't they you end up repeating the same thing again and again, because that's the way we've always done things. It's not until somebody from the outside comes in and says "why are you doing it like that?" That's a really good resource for people to get in to. Do you just request to join that Facebook group?

Rob Fox: Yes absolutely. Send that request in on Facebook. Currently we are at 750 people on there, but looking to expand. It started initially with myself and Wendy Baker setting this up. But now she's left the group to me to manage things. So now it's just myself currently running the group. I look forward to hearing your insights and sharing share with you.

Kathy Brodie: Absolutely. That link for the Facebook page is there on the website now so just click through to that and that'll take you straight through to Rob's Facebook page there so you can see out any discussions.

That might be about being a young male in the industry sorts of things that you might have come across. And if you are a young male in the industry and you maybe want to ask some of those questions I'm sure Rob take direct messages as well, if there's something you don't want to put on a public forum because obviously that's quite public isn't it.

Rob Fox: Absolutely. I'm more than willing to accept requests private messages and if you've got any concerns or want to discuss if you're having any problems as male within the industry and the right people to talk to you more they're willing to offer those introductions as well.

Kathy Brodie: Thank you so much Rob. It's always interesting to have a different perspective, especially somebody that's just starting out in the industry and how you view the sector as it is now. So thank you very much indeed for joining us today Rob Fox.

Rob Fox: Thank you very much Kathy.

CHAPTER 7

THE TRANSITION FROM RECEPTION YEAR INTO YEAR ONE

Alistair Bryce-Clegg

Kathy Brodie: I'm thrilled to be joined by the irrepressible Alistair Bryce-Clegg. Alistair had a successful 10 year career as a head teacher of a three form entry infant school and Early Years unit in Cheshire. Alongside his headship he established a consultancy career specializing in the education of children in the Early Years.

Demand for his consultancy became so great that Alistair left the headship and established ABCdoes which you can find on the Internet under www.abcdoes.com. Most of his time is spent supporting practitioners in their settings or delivering key notes and training specializing in all areas of Early Years practice and management for both the maintained and non maintained sectors and Alistair does that both nationally and internationally.

He's also an award winning author and product designer. His work's been published in a number of books and magazines and he gets to sit on the advisory board for the Early Years Educator magazine. Alongside support and training for a range of schools and settings, Alistair also works internationally with local authorities everywhere around the world really. So welcome to the summit, Alistair Bryce-Clegg.

Alistair Bryce-Clegg: What an introduction! That was great.

Kathy Brodie: Today we're going to be looking at transitions and particularly how that affects children's personal, social and emotional development and the area of transition I'd like to discuss today is from Reception to Year One.

In England, this is quite a significant move because it's a change in curricula, they're moving from the Early Years Foundation Stage (EYFS) into Key Stage 1, which is very often a more formal learning environment. This can mean big changes for children and in particular their personal, social and emotional development. So could you just talk a little bit about that transition first and how we can support children's personal, social emotional development during this big transition time for them.

Alistair Bryce-Clegg: It is a massive time of transition, although the Early Years Foundation Stage has been in place quite a long time now and we have a National Curriculum, we've made lots of changes to our approach to Early Years education. In lots of settings I work with transition projects or just Year One staff or Reception staff looking at their transition, that actual transition itself in a lot of settings has changed massively but also a lot has not changed very much at all.

The transition still ends up being a couple of story swaps in the last couple of weeks of term or the joint assembly or the odd visit here and there. Then we have five or six weeks off away from school and then "bam!" we're back into Year One. Lots of children will have been used to a more play based approach in the Foundation Stage, lots of opportunities for self selection, continuous provision, outdoor access. Because of the pressure that is put on Year One teachers and because of the understanding of Year One they move into things like carpet sessions, 50 minutes literacy followed by literacy activity followed by playtime followed by maths activities followed by lunch time and then topic in the afternoon.

A lot of Year One teachers work extremely hard and are run ragged trying to get through the wealth of stuff they've got to get through in terms of the curriculum, with massive pressure: You've got your Year One phonics checker on the horizon, you have to get children through that. Then they have massive frustration at some of those children are not able to keep up with that pace and that rigour.

That's not always, as we found through the transition projects, as you'd expect your children who are less well-developed at this stage. Often we think it's those children - your left handed, August born boys - who may well struggle in this transition period and undoubtedly a lot of them do. Being the father of three boys, one of whom is a left handed, August born boy, I can speak from experience. We found during the transition project, on a number of projects we've done, often some of the more able children also really suffered socially and emotionally from transition. This had a massive impact on their attainment and that was a bit of a surprise for everybody taking part in the project.

But the emotional well-being (and it's not when you think about it) the children's emotional wellbeing can have such a huge impact on their ability to attain because when you are not comfortable, when we're not secure, you are going back into that kind of more reptilian brain you're a little bit more in flight or fight. You are not sitting there thinking "I'm here to answer absorb every moment of what's happening".

When we interviewed the children, which we did as part of the project, about what are you looking forward to before you transition and then during and after, what you found 'different' (never what don't you like but what you found different) and the things that were coming up, that were really important came up all the time. Things like:

lack of outdoor provision

when was it time to go outdoors

when was it time to choose or play

But even things like the toilet - I don't like going to the toilet because you have to go down the corridor in the toilet and I don't like the toilets, they're different.

Where do you put your pencil? I used to have a tray, I used to have a drawer with all my things in it. Now I haven't.

Even the little things that change the dynamic of the room or the dynamic of routine. That's kind of what got in the way.

It's about saying to Early Years staff - most of the time it's not about you. You can be the loveliest, most gorgeous teacher on the planet and that will go a long way to make most children feel valued and secure. But when we are transitioning, it's the unfamiliarity that gets in the way - the environments, you, the routine and that in itself has a massive impact on what we do and how they do it.

So, the more you can make the unfamiliar, familiar, the more opportunity there is for children to feel that they have high level of wellbeing and therefore the more open they are to change. That sounds really simple, in essence it is, but it's also extremely complex.

In an ideal transition, you want Year One to be far more like Reception than you do Reception becoming like Year One in the first term. Again, it is very common especially in primary schools, where they say, "Right, you've had enough time faffing about in the sand and water. It's the third term let's get the sand and water outside. Let's get some tables in. Let's get a little bit more rigour" (which is what an interesting term, there is no rigour in play, there's only rigour when it comes to sitting down at a table with a worksheet or a book or sitting on the carpet).

We know nationally even now, although the good levels of development is increasing, there are still roughly a third of children nationally who didn't achieve a good level of development by the end of the Foundation Stage. So, that third of children transitioned into Year One, still not at a stage that was appropriate for their age at the end of a play based Foundation Stage.

So if you take those children, who are probably the most vulnerable ones, and then give them a curriculum that is much, much faster paced - sitting down on the carpet, very controlled, direct teaching - they are not going to flourish. If they didn't flourish in that more developmentally appropriate curriculum Foundation Stage, they are not going to flourish in Year One.

They are going to be the children that spend their entire academic life in the Sunshine Room with a lady in a tabard, to do an intervention before they get rolled back into the classroom. When actually, if we just have a little more developmentally appropriate curriculum on entry to Year One the child would begin to make big strides forward.

Normally our transition projects take at least two years, if not three. So we look at current practice, then do a year's training, then transition and then do a year's evaluation of the transition. But in schools where we changed the transition process (and again that comes with its complications) where we had Year One that operated more like a good Foundation Stage approach - I stress the term *good*, it wasn't just a case of saying, right in Year One, we'll have a sand and water tray and a role play area and saying to the children, "what do you fancy doing? well off you go and do it" - there was that rigour.

So, we were looking at good continuous provision. We were looking at environments that were linked to day to day assessment. We were looking at challenges in the environment. The role of the adult.

How observation and assessment is still a really effective tool in Year One.

How you can look at the Year One curriculum and break it down into skills as opposed to be modules and that you can take those skills into a very Foundation Stage way of planning.

How you can do cross phase planning, where you can have elements of EY outcomes from Development Matters and also into the National Curriculum within one planning format.

Looking at mechanisms like staggered entry to continuous provision where different children have to focus my good provision at slightly different times, allowing some children who need more support to get that support.

It's really more of a stress to get that stretch.

So there were lots of things that we looked at. We found the attainment of all children, including the more able, were significantly better when there was a more Foundation Stage approach on entry to Year One. But it was unpicking that with practitioners, the fact that we're not just talking about four corners and that we know you've got less staff.

We know you probably haven't got outdoor access, we know you've got to keep your tables and chairs in here because at some point everybody will sit down they have lunch served in here. It's not just about that.

It's about fundamental principles of what makes transition effective. It's like when we start a new job in a new school or a new setting and it's your first day in, you've been in the interview, which was nerve-wracking, you've taken a quick look around, you've met the team. They are lovely. The lady from the office has phoned you up about payroll. She was lovely. You get excited about going because it's a new start and you want to be there.

But on day one, when you are going into that staffroom you're not quite sure where you sit, whose cup is whose, do you bring your own tea or coffee. You're not quite sure how to get up and down the corridor when the bell rings at play time or what exactly happens. That is like a child going into Year One - it is familiar but really unfamiliar.

So on that first day although you are lovely and everybody else is lovely you are not on top of your game because you are taking time to find out how it all works. When you are secure in how it all works, then you begin to become *you*. What we found at transition a lot of children are not secure in how it works on entry to Year One so they're not massively open to learning, so then that's when they underperform.

So you get a lot of Year One teachers who, rightly so, look at children who have been assessed at one level or come up with the GLD that's really good and looking at this child and thinking, "this paper tells me you're at a good level of development and I'm looking at your examples of mark making and I'm seeing here this annotated work that shows you actually were able to write in a sentence and demarcate it correctly. When I'm asking you to do the same task, where's all that learning gone? How come it's leaked out your ear overnight?".

There is still a little bit of tension sometimes between Year One teachers and Reception teachers where Year One teachers are looking at children saying this is not the child I am looking at on paper.

The way we got round that in the project was that across the year, not just in the summer term, but in autumn term, spring term and summer term, Year One and Reception started joint moderation. Don't just leave it. We try to get the Year One staff to come into Early Years in the Autumn term to see what they are like on point of entry because you will know, and people watching and listening to this will know, as a Reception teacher like every year group, you get to the end of the year, you love them like you've never loved a class before.

Then come September you are literally crying in your stock

cupboard, saying "they weren't this bad last year, this is the worst year we've ever had. Half of them can't line up, they can't sit on the carpet, we're never going to get them to where we need them to be" and so its really good for Year One staff to come and see that.

See what Early Years children look like at the very beginning of the Early Years process. But then in the Spring to look at those children again and in the Summer to look at those children again and do some joint moderation of things like mark making or mathematics or personal, social interaction.

The key that we used are the Leuven Scales, which I know are very popular and widely used. I know you're going to be talking about them on the Summit, which is great. Initially when we first did the transition projects, we use the Leuven Scales as our marker. We didn't use any academic attainment at all in the first project, we only used social and emotional well-being as the marker of how children are transitioning.

As I've done that with other groups of schools and other local authorities they have requested that we then put in an academic marker, rather than just social and emotional wellbeing marker and I think that's just a sign of where we are in terms of education that social emotional well-being is not enough. We need some academic rigour in there.

Now of course we've got SSTEW which a lot of Early Years settings are using in-line with ITERS and ECERS that also, like the Leuven Scales can work very well when looking at a transition.

But our basic premise was that we took six children from each Reception class that were a sample and we looked at them in the Summer term and we asked for a mixture of boys, girls, SEN, high ability children it's just a real mix. We got the Reception and the Year One teacher together, after some training, to carry out a Leuven Scale of wellbeing and involvement on those six children.

So each of those six children, when they felt at their most secure in the Summer term in Reception, were given a Leuven score for wellbeing and Leuven score for involvement. Latterly, we then also collected in an example of mark making, an attainment statement in terms for where they were in terms of mathematics, a reading level for some schools and a general statement of that child's how they work within the set.

Then we go off on our summer holidays. In the first year of the transition project we'd then we come back, having transitioned in the way that schools have always transitioned, which could be a couple of shared stories sessions.

Then about three weeks in, they were Leuven Scaled again by the same two staff (or if a member of staff had moved or was off on maternity leave the other Year One teacher). And what we looked at in that first transition is "Do children in their state of well-being and involvement stay the same, go up or reduce".

All of the projects, every single one, the majority of children, like 98 per cent of children, will drop at least one scale points in one of the Leuven Scales.

Some children dropped up to *four* scale points, just on transition, just in terms of wellbeing.

Then what we did was to Leuven scale them every term thereafter (or some schools did it every half term, but mostly it was every term) to see how long it took for children to reclaim that.

Some within the first half term are back to where they were. They were usually but not always, your high scorers anyway. Where children have dropped a lot of points or where children really struggled to make up for Scale points were usually your more vulnerable ones, the ones that aren't reaching the GLD, especially boys who have no access to outdoors etc. etc.

In every single project it took some children (albeit a minority, but they are still significant because they are some children) a whole year just to get back to where they were in terms of wellbeing and involvement. So you got some children who take an academic year to get back to a state where they feel as secure and engaged as they were an academic year ago.

That's the worry because they tend to be the children who are more vulnerable anyway, that tend to be a children who haven't reached their good level of development anyway, they tend to be the children who are more physically literate and so therefore *need* a more play based approach, need more access to the outdoors. But in terms of attainment for the school or for the child they become children who don't attain well.

Where, actually, if they were given a more appropriate curriculum if they were given more effective transition, they would begin to attain far, far better, their progress will be better, their self-esteem would be better, their attainment would be better.

So again, as I said before, we had gorgeous Year One teachers who worked incredibly hard trying tie up all their ends and make everything fit and still. These children in their care were dropping in back in the Leuven Scale, were not making the academic progress to meet where they had been at the end of Reception and that was because it felt very unfamiliar within that space.

Kathy Brodie: So do you do research then and have a look to see those had transitioned successfully or when you changed that transition process what happened then with their Leuven Scales and SSTEW scales and so on.

Alistair Bryce-Clegg: What we did then was unpicked and look at those children who haven't dropped any points in terms of well-being and involvement. And we looked at those children in terms of their academic profile but also their social, emotional profile.

And they tended to be on the whole girls, not exclusively but primarily girls, and they also tended to be girls who, when you discussed a kind of profile within the group tended to be leaders, tend to be ones who were quite socially emotionally secure within the group. They fell into a quite a typical category, most of them. They were quite secure and often were described by the Reception staff as children who were 'ready for the National Curriculum'.

And actually that would be a two edged sword, because we all know what that means, but if your Foundation Stage approach is good - for me you can run a Foundation Stage approach from birth through to Year 6 and, if that was done well, you would still challenge those children, they would still make progress. It wouldn't look exactly the same in Year 6 is does in Reception, but the elements would be there.

And interestingly I worked with a couple of schools who are doing just that, who are running that Foundation Stage ethos right the way through primary and getting some really interesting results, especially but not exclusively, with more vulnerable learners.

Also Upstart Scotland, who are a movement trying to get the academic school starting age in Scotland moved to 7 have got their own website which is just Upstart Scotland, but on there they publish lots of really interesting academic research. A couple of months ago they published a paper which is about more able children in a play based environment. So, do more able children need a more academic environment to thrive academically or can they thrive *academically* in a play based environment.

It was carried out by the University of Strathclyde or Aberdeen (it was one of the two) and the findings were fascinating, that actually children in a more play based environment, even the very,

very academic children, did better than children of similar academic standards that were given a formal environment.

Of course there are lots of subtleties to what that play based environment looked like, how they were going to be challenged within that. It's just interesting that often, and I know it's often not the teacher, it can be senior leaders, it can be Ofsted, who think that unless they're sitting down doing something focussed and formal and they can't be learning.

Actually, high level engagement gives you high level of attainment and our high level engagement comes mainly through play but of course play (which is a different Summit altogether!) can be interpreted in many different ways. Play is not just about stickle bricks on the carpet. But it can be. Adults engage in play. Adults learn best in play. Sometimes we learn best through stickle bricks and on the carpet, but the type of play that we're talking about is just that high level engagement

It's that thing I talk about a lot in my work which is Thrill, Will, Skill where: If there is no thrill, there is no will to take part. If there's no will to take part, then you don't acquire a skill. A thrill doesn't have to be "Ta-Da" - its just something I am interested in. For an adult, it's just finding that book that you want to read, find that magazine. It's about finding that YouTube clip that's interesting or funny that makes you want to find out more. And that's play - that is play. You find that element and it's the enjoyment for you, outside of the rigour and mundane and that's what we need to get lots more.

So then we started to unpick even further and say - Well how can we try and keep an element of rigour through play? How can we make this transition in more effective transitions so the children aren't dropping their Scale points? So again, in the second year of the cycle of our transition projects, we then are working all year on mechanisms to effective a transition. So, the transition process would start any time from October half term. It starts literally coming in September (depends if you have staggered intake) from October half term, elements of transition start to plop in.

From that point for me any visits from members of staff who are in the Year One team (and I can't guarantee that whoever is in Year One this year is going to be Year One next year, and I'm not expecting you to) but what you are saying is, this person is coming in, starting talking about Year One, we might pop up to Year One and have a visit, depending where you might you be geographically.

But more importantly for transition was that we were saying "OK, When those children transition from Reception into a Year One, even though we've not done a year's work on transition, we would like some staff who are familiar faces, whether it be the support staff or the teaching staff". You can, if you're a staggered entry into your Reception, don't start that staggered entry until maybe a week in the first week of term. The Reception staff go into Year One and are in and out all day, every day, across this first week. That gives a real sense of security.

And interestingly, we also talked to parents about the transition project and parent's anxiety about transition is often quite high. Although they're keen for children get into school they don't know how it's going to be, how it's going to be different. When parents saw a familiar face in the classroom, albeit teaching staff or a TA from Reception, it massively quelled their anxiety which then had an impact on their children.

Often as well in Year One, because the geography of the school and how your day works, and the timetable, often in the Early Years its - doors open, everybody piles in, Buggy's, adults, aunties, Grandma... Because you've often have a higher staff ratio, if somebody says "Can I just ask....", (it's never ideal) you can say "of course you can" or "come and catch me at the end of the day." A bit of nattering goes on as the children are settling in.

Often in Year One, we pick them up from the playground waiting outside the door. Suddenly for the parents that connection also stops and that gives them anxiety. So we looked at Reception staff been there. Some schools transitioned a Reception teacher to be the Year One teacher, some transitioned a support member of staff from Reception into Year One and they did a cycle of year on, year off in the Reception and Year One, so they got really in-depth knowledge around Year One.

Some just had them there in the beginning to welcome the children into register time and then disappeared. That made a big difference.

We tried to get the Reception staff to visit the Year One staff and see children in action, so the Reception could say "gosh, look how you've come on, look what you doing now". They could also say "well, I wouldn't have had her next to him". That was useful and the staff found that during talk time, whilst they are trying to settle the children down, it was really good to have a member of staff who knows those children to come in and say "they need a bit of nurture".

That worked really well and then we got the Year One staff to go to Reception and see how those children come in, from the very beginning from the October half term.

We tried to get them to diarise that, so we said every term in the diary they either did a swap where one went to Reception and they swapped, so no supply costs were needed. In an ideal scenario on one day the Reception teacher on one morning (or one afternoon) went to Year One and they shared together to team teach and then in the other day, they went into Reception, so you can actually chat with each other about each others concern but then of course there's a cost involved in that. Just seeing it made a massive difference, staff swapping made a massive difference.

Then we started working on opportunities for children then to visit Year One in small groups or larger groups. One of the schools we worked with did a really effective project where they had a group of buddies from Year One who came down to Early Years. When they came down to the Early Years, the Early Years children knew they were coming, at carpet time, at the end of the day and the Reception had come up with questions they would like to ask the buddies and the buddies came and answered those questions.

The Reception asked daft things like "do you have construction" and "where do you put your snack" but also the Year One buddies came and said "It's ace in Year One. You gonna love it. We don't have this, but we have that, you don't do this, you do that, and you get to go here". So they really sold it as children as been this really exciting thing to do, "It's good, it's Fantastic".

All of these things trying to work on children's self-esteem and anxiety so that they weren't thinking "oh no", because often we'll say things as parents like it's 'Big School'. That language that we use, make children nervous about big school, in you've got to do 'proper work' all this kind of language that we come out with, or parents will.

The other big thing we did was to, apart from the ongoing assessment, was to look at the role of parents, so they should be really well informed. A lot of the schools did something either during school time or after the school day where they invited small groups of parents to come to school in groups of 10. Come with your child into the Year One environment and to meet the Year One staff.

The Year One environment was often set up as it would be for point of entry so it looked a lot more like a Foundation Stage setting. They then would say, one member of staff is going to have a chat with the parents, while the other members staff works with the children and shows them round the space, maybe does a story or an activity. The parents have then got an opportunity to ask any questions they want to ask.

Staff can then say, this is what we do. Also a lot of schools was got out examples (for academic achievement) of where children were in their reading and their writing and their maths by the end of Year One. So the teachers could say "Yes, this is the approach we use, here are examples of where our children end up" because a lot of parent's concern was "I love the fact that they play. I love the fact that they're nurtured BUT if they play for another year when are they ever going to learn". Again, it just can be a very misinformed parent, that you're not learning while in the Foundation Stage, but the ability of the Year One staff to see "we do this because socially and emotionally it's much better for these children. But actually this is what you can achieve through a really effective, slightly more child led very engaging play base approach".

So that made a big difference and because they were coming in in small groups, they felt they got to ask their question as opposed to just - which can be valid - kind of mass presentation that you might do to parents in an evening after school.

Kathy Brodie: That's a more traditional way of doing it - to have all the parents in, you'd have that transition meeting. This is where you hang your coat, you're not allowed in the class room anymore, don't bring peanut butter in, any all that sort of thing.

Alistair Bryce-Clegg: You've got to get all that information across, but it's often a bit about: We don't do that now, you need this. It's about trying to find a happy balance.

But, what we found fundamentally was in all of the transition projects that we've done, and in the work with individual schools (and it's hard because other things get in the way - SEN meetings, lost pump bags, time moves on, school productions) - but when your focus is on transition, you've also got a lot of training to do.

Some Year One staff, who have never taught in Foundation Stage, are not familiar with how the Foundation Stage works, not familiar with the play based approach. When we talk to them their panic was "you're going to make me play in the sand all day and I'll never get my teaching done" or they would say "no I'm quite happy to do that but I'm not quite sure what it is I'm supposed to be doing. How do you..." Because if you don't work in Foundation Stage it's full of jargon, it's full of terminology it's full of things like your continuous provision, what on earth is that? you've got enhancements to your continuous provision, you got your direct teaching, non-direct teaching, adult supported learning, observation, assessment, peer observing.... what are all these things that we talk about all the time? And so you suddenly say to somebody in Year One, who has never taught that, right when they come in September, can we have continuous provision, proper continuous provision, not just four corners, and can you work and integrated day, where you're looking at your whole class input but then adults in supporting your observations and assessment.... No wonder you've got somebody saying "Hey, hang on a minute! I need to get my head around it"

If you are going to have effective transitioning, then Year One staff need a really good idea of what effective Early Years Foundation Stage provision looks like.

Where we do go slightly awry, is when some Year One staff, with no experience but are very willing, misinterpreted Early Years provision as just being construction, painting easel, role play and then children did 'focused work' and went off to there once you'd finished your work and had a good time. But actually it wasn't good continuous provision and therefore attainment in those settings did dip a bit, until we went back and looked and said - well when they leave you, what exactly is it that they are doing, and this provision you put out. How is it linked to their next steps?

When we got that sorted out then it popped up a bit but it can be a little bit of a dangerous time if children are just going into quite low level, free choice after you've finished your work.

It's going to be an ethos of a Foundation Stage approach to child initiated learning through continuous provision. So that takes time and that takes training. But, undoubtedly, when they got it right, and nobody ever gets it completely right, but when they found an understanding, we saw in ALL settings, not only did levels of wellbeing and involvement increase - but also academic progress. Because children were feeling more secure, staff had a better understanding and we saw an increase in all children especially in more vulnerable, lower third who dipped in their GLD.

So the second half of our transition project are the ones where we've put transition in for a year. We then go back to Reception and say right, this is the second year, let's get our six children, let's do our Leuven Scales together - Year One and Reception. Let's take our five, six weeks holiday. Let's come back three weeks in. Let's go again.

And what we found was in the second year of the cycle some children drop a point or two in some areas, the biggest drop we ever got was two points - as a posed to it being four points.

BUT, then what we found was usually by Christmas the majority - the vast majority - are back to where they were. So easily, within a term, in they'd found their feet and were back in line with where they were, as opposed to some of them being 12 months later back in line. We know their social, emotional wellbeing is high instead of insecure, then their ability to absorb, to engage, to learn, and to explore is going to happen.

As you can probably tell, I'm quite passionate about effective transition. Because it's not just about the social, emotional wellbeing of children, it's also about social, emotional wellbeing of adults. I work with Year One teachers who've got such a vast amount of pressure on them. People who will say things like - You need to get hit the ground running. You need to pull them by the bootstraps. Time to get some work done. They feel an immense amount of pressure. They have to get them ready, because they've got Year 2 coming up, SATS within Year 2. So you've then got stressed teachers and very stressed teachers, no matter what year group they're in, don't make for very relaxed children.

If you're stressed and feel pressure, the children are going to be stressed and feel the pressure. But if you are secure that you've got a plan and then actually you've got happy staff, and happy staff make for happy children, make effective learners. That's what we're aiming for.

An effective play based transition, giving children developmentally appropriate curriculum and in developmentally appropriate environment, then will give you developmentally appropriate results which means children will make good progress.

And I am secure in that, having done the amount of project work that I've done now, and the amount of work in schools that I've worked with, I am very secure in the knowledge that an effective transition process gives you far better outcomes.

Maybe not initially - you're not seeing the fact they've got a piece of work in the book every week, which is their diary entry about what they did at the weekend. Maybe you don't get that in the initial half-term term, but what you'll get is children with a genuine passion and interest in writing, boys who are keen to make marks, as well as talk, as well as socially interact. So it does benefit for the majority of children.

Kathy Brodie: I think the research is fascinating behind it, in many ways it's very intuitive is kind of what you'd expect. It's interesting that there were some dramatic effects and that the scale points were so different.

So what I'm hearing is that this is a whole setting thing, that there isn't just one way the one practitioner could do transitions like this, that really has got to be thought about with the whole school and with Reception with Year One and even perhaps further up the school as well. So what could one practitioner in a setting maybe do to start this ball rolling?

Alistair Bryce-Clegg: A really interesting place to start is where the research starts. You're not just one lonely practitioner coming in saying "I had a really good idea - why don't we just play all day in Year One?" The feedback we got - because we involved head teachers, governors, parents in all of the project we've done - but also got lots of e-mails from Year One teachers saying either "my school has asked me to have a more play based approach in year one" or more often "I've got these group of children, just come into Year one. They seem to really need that play based approach. But I am at a loss to how I can do that and get what my senior 'leadersheep' are asking for - leadership not 'leadersheep' that was a bit of an Freudian slip - and then they are being observed and I'm really worried about having play going on in that space".

So, it's always good to come from a research angle to say that there is lots of information out there, not just about transition but about (and the summit is going to be one thing that talks about how children social emotional wellbeing ultimately impacts on every aspect of them as a person) and therefore their learning and therefore their interaction with other people. So if you get that bit right the learning bit, which is secondary really to feeling like a valued, well-adjusted, happy person will come.

So there are lot of books around about transition - I've got a book about transition about to come out, on my blog the ABCdoes.com there are a couple of transition projects on there, one from Blackpool one from Salford you can download and have a look at. It's got all the numbers and the data that went along with it and also comments from staff and from head teachers.

One of the biggest battles I had was just the convincing people that you can learn through play. And I think that's a fundamental issue that we have in Early Years in education anyway, not just with senior leadership team, but with the government and people making decisions about how we operate as schools - that you can get high attainment from a really good play based approach, it doesn't have to be linked to sitting on the carpet or worksheets.

So if I was going to look at effective transition as a Year One teacher, that's where I would come from. I'd try and get skilled up as much as I could, in terms of that kind of research and go and say, look this can happen. It *can* happen.

If you are a Reception teacher whose been frustrated because you know that some of your children need, in fact all of your children, need a continuum of that play based approach. But maybe the person being fed into you, as lovely as they are, is not very aware of that particular pedagogy and goes down a more static line, then I think it's also about a little bit of trial and error about trying some initiatives, about looking at things like joint moderation, by trying to get in things like observation, and going at it slowly because you just happened to chip, chip, chip, away.

If you have vastly radical approach where you say, "Right, from September no tables in Year One, all play based" and the Year One team are not secure in that, or the senior leadership team aren't secure in that, then it's going to fall apart.

One of the things that one Year One teacher described in one of the projects was she thought she was 'free falling' when she first started the first year because she had a complete lack of control. She was used to saying on day one session one it's this and this is what we do and then I planned five activities that they go on to, then we come back together. We do an assessment of you, then we go on. She said "I literally feel like I have lost control".

What was interesting, as part of the project, that we were able to give support go in and observe and by October half term she was then saying "No, I get the hang of it now. What felt like free fall before actually feels like an opportunity to be able to go and teach as opposed to just deliver", which is a nice thing to say but having a team that are appreciative that you might have a little wobble and it might all feel very new and insecure. That's to be expected, so not expected to fail but, in the knowledge that, if you try something new and it's a significant change and you're dealing with lots of personalities, not just one but a whole team, then there are going to be hiccups along the way.

But talk about those, go back to the research, seek out people who've done it before. Ask them the questions which is the wonder of the Internet. There's always somebody out there somewhere who's done something similar. Be able to give you some pointers and then go back and try again.

It is very much a community approach. Parents need to be involved and not think that "Oh, our children are playing again". Governors need to be involved, so they really back the initiative, because if you are going to introduce play based learning in Year One, the chances are you might need some slightly different furniture, you might need some slightly different resources because you won't be resourced for play. You are more likely to be resourced for more formal types of learning. So they need to be on board in terms of funding and agreement.

Then the whole staff team need to appreciate - you don't want somebody in Year Six going "You are kidding me!! They're playing for a whole year in Reception and now they are playing for another year, in Year One. Are we ever going to get the work done?!"

Kathy Brodie: And as you said, there is research out there and there's certainly lots of people writing about the benefits of play and so on. I know your Facebook group there's very often discussions going on about people who are trying the play based approach and with lots of practical ideas about "this is how I've tried it". Both your website and your Facebook page I think are great resources to go and find some of that information and share some of those kind of maybe frustrations or of course the successes - I've tried this and this is what's happened.

So there's masses of information there. What would your top tip be? You're a practitioner sitting here watching this, listening to this thinking "that sounds perfect, that would absolutely fit my pedagogy. This is something I really want to try." What would your top tip be for that practitioner?

Alistair Bryce-Clegg: Go with your gut. I think it's my ultimate top tip for anybody who is working with children. If you are feeling like there is immense amount of pressure coming from here, there's immense pressure coming from there, but when I sit in front of those children, I know that with the best will in the world I am not giving them what they need, then go with your gut and go and seek out the research that's out there go and seek out the anecdotal stuff that's out there.

The great thing about things like Facebook forums (although they can have the downfalls) and Twitter discussions is that rather than some expert on a summit telling you what they should do, you actually hear somebody who does it on a daily basis who says "right I was really sceptical. I tried it. It went disastrously wrong then I tried it again and it's been the best thing I've ever done".

So always, if that little voice is saying to you "this is not right this doesn't feel right" especially that little group of children (often boys, but not always) that are having to leave you again for their intervention, to come back when the whole group is moved on, that's when you think there are numerous settings out there, that have taken that kind of scenario and turned it on its head.

So settings I've worked with in Reception and Foundation Stage where children came out of reception with a 23, 24 per cent Good Level of Development (GLD) and got into a more play based approach in Year One, where everybody was panic stricken that if they played again you would never get the GLD up for these children. Seriously, the groundwork has been done and they are showing that they are ready and they begin to fly. And then they get in terms of academic results, the best results the schools have ever seen for that age group, but actually much more important is fundamentally a personal social wellbeing. They are happy children and happy children make successful learners.

Kathy Brodie: As well as all the moral obligations that we have to these children and their childhood as well. But as you say from a school point of view, this is when they're going to achieve - when they're happy and when they're a good personal social emotional place.

Alistair Bryce-Clegg: Fundamentally, that never sits well with me, the fact that we always talk about children in terms of their outcomes. Because the education system is such that we talk about "they got the best results", when actually the fundamental thing is we are looking after children, nurturing their wellbeing.

If we want happy, successful, well-balanced adults to create a happy successful well-balanced society, it's our job to get it right really early on, because it doesn't always happen at home, it doesn't always happen in the community. In school or whatever setting you are in, it is a safe haven been where you are there and your primary role, I always think, regardless of whether they can read and write or whatever, is to make them feel valued, supported and safe. I think when that's in place then the other will come.

So we are judged wrongly I think by our academic achievements. Actually it's the fundamental principle of wellbeing that will get children to wherever they need to be.

Kathy Brodie: Couldn't agree more. you've mentioned you have a book about transitions into Year One that's published by Bloomsbury and that's out in the Spring 2017 and that'll be available both on Bloomsbury and on Amazon for people to pre-order or to buy straightaway.

Your blog post is www.abcdoes.com - lots and lots of blogs on there - lots of lovely pictures as well as have a bit of a scroll through and see what's happening. So yeah I do go and visit that. As always an absolute pleasure to speak with the Alistair Bryce-Clegg. Good advice. Really excited to hear about the research in the work as you say that's three or four years worth of work that you've condensed there for us, so do appreciate you doing that.

Thank you very much indeed for joining us on the Early Years Web Summit, Alistair Bryce-Clegg.

Alistair Bryce-Clegg: Thank you.

CHAPTER 8

THE PHOENIX CUPS PHILOSOPHY

Sandi Phoenix

Kathy Brodie: I am thrilled to be joined from Australia by Sandi Phoenix. Sandi is a founding company director and principal facilitator at Phoenix support for educators. She is highly regarded as a speaker, coach, mentor and Professional Development Facilitator for the education and care sector in Australia. Sandi is well known for her 'Phoenix Cups Philosophy' that has revolutionized the way that educators understand and support children's behavioural learning. This concept has recently been developed into a resource, the Phoenix Cups kit, which is now available for educators. I'm hoping we will get to look at that at the end of the interview here. Welcome to the Early Years Web Summit Sandi Phoenix.

Sandi Phoenix: Thank you so much Kathy. I'll be excited to show you about that. We're all pretty pumped about it around here and it's so good to be here at this Summit with you. I watched it last year and it was exciting stuff. So I'm really glad to be a part of it.

Kathy Brodie: This is going to be really interesting to hear about something brand new. I've certainly never seen the cups before so this is going to be really, really interesting for me as well. We're looking particularly on this Summit at personal, social and emotional development. So can we start by discussing a bit about children's sense of well-being in a setting - whether that's a child minder or day care or any other setting. What can we do in these settings to help children's well-being?

Sandi Phoenix: My key advice, I think that I live by constantly, is let's just follow those children's leads. We really don't need to have some amazing insight and have read 50,000 textbooks on anatomy and children's development to know what they need to meet their own needs for wellbeing at any point in time. The children are magically wired to do what they need to do to fulfil their sense of well-being at any point in time.

What we can do is mess that up by interrupting and interfering with children's natural movements. At that point, we have to start to compensate and work out where we've gone wrong and we just need to back off a bit.

If we just watch what's happening, we actually look - for example, we really don't need to know exactly when upper body strength is going to start to be developed. We see children start to hang off monkey bars or hang off anything that their parents don't want them to hang off. And often break things in that way! Hang their body upside down, pull it all the way up. When we say "go for it - let me facilitate that. How can I resource this space to help with your learning?" then that well-being just happens.

When we say "Stop! Don't do that, sit down over here and open this book" for example, then we're going to start to get interruptions with the child's sense of well-being because their development is being disrupted.

One last thing that I always say is, if you're confused or you're not sure about how to create this space for the child to develop properly, then just plonk them outside. That's all we need to do! Put children outside, that's where they develop best. Children can experience all the seven senses and start to integrate those senses. There is natural resources, loose parts, there's things to climb off, swing off and throw and lift and pull and push and amazing things happen.

I think where we're starting to find issues with this is when we put children in captivity and we hold them in four walls all day and then we say "I wonder what's wrong with them?"

That's my hot tip - just to let them do what they've got to do.

Kathy Brodie: I noticed you said the using the *seven* senses. Can you tell us about the extra two senses because we normally talk about the five senses. What are the extra two senses you're talking about?

Sandi Phoenix: Thanks for asking. I guess there are many different theoretical frameworks that throw in a couple or two. You know Montessori has some, Steiner has some. This is from a biological perspective we're talking about two scientifically known senses of proprioception and vestibular.

Children know when they need to develop, for example, their vestibular sense because they start to exercise their ability to balance. They look for opportunities to balance - and usually risky opportunities where parents and educators and carers are saying "Get down from there! Don't balance on that!" but the child is just saying "I'm just exercising my vestibular system. Please don't touch me". And if we don't touch them, then their vestibular system develops nicely. Of course we need to throw some crash mats underneath in case they fall or support them to do their own risk analysis.

Proprioception and vestibular are good things to know about. Thank goodness for Google. I don't have to talk long about it. You can research it!

Kathy Brodie: It's really interesting the way that all these all the different senses all come together like that!

I know that you talk a lot about challenging behaviour. How would you describe challenging behaviour and what sort of things do you hear from educators and practitioners about challenging behaviour?

Sandi Phoenix: First of all, I tend not use the term challenging behaviour. I often say to educators "tell me about the behaviour that challenges *you*" because let's be real, what challenges one person, the next person calls spirited. The things that challenge me are often really different things that challenge my colleagues and vice versa. So those behaviours that just push our buttons for our own reasons. We really have to own that and understand why.

But then when we look deeper at that behaviour that's challenging an educator, I often hear about aggression as being one of those things that is at the top of the responses that I'm going to work on. I'm responding to aggressive behaviour in childcare services all of the time, because that's where it becomes an exclusion risk. That's where there is this duty of care to the other 30 children. A lot of the time as an inclusion support role I'm coming in to support that child who's displaying these aggressive behaviours to try and work out how to be a part of this community a little better.

Often what I see, when I'm watching the child who's being the aggressive one (and that can be really ambiguous) but let's say he's punching, hitting, kicking and spitting, often I see irritability and a lot of that time that irritability is happening indoors. So again, I'm a huge advocate for let's get him outside, because I'm often told it doesn't really happen outside's or if it does, it happens right before the transition to inside - because he knows that he's only been allowed to go outside for 45 minutes and now he has come in again.

Kathy Brodie: For some challenging behaviour, what happens is they actually have their play time taken away - you're not going to go outside and play! Ooops, have I panicked you?

Sandi Phoenix: Oh my goodness, these poor children. Yes! That's exactly what happens! I notice this in our culture, particularly in schools. That's quite likely to happen in primary schools. When it's happened to my boys in the past I've had things to say about it!

I can see as educators and teachers trying to just get a handle on things and try to have some control over the situation and will use that as this kind of 'time out'. But it's not effective, it actually doesn't work. If it worked then there'd be evidence behind it and it'd be written into our policies and we'd be doing it. But it actually doesn't work. So we need to do the opposite. And just saying "it looks like you need some time outside. You go out and you have *two* lunch breaks today". That would be more effective.

It's quite shocking to me that we treat children quite differently than the way we treat adults. We work down here in what we call the dungeon, which is our office suites that are underground, and we can't see outside, there's no windows. So often one of us will say "OK I'm just feeling really agitated. I need to go and see the sunlight". If one of my employees said that and I just kind of took that away from her or him and said "No, I don't think you will actually. You're going to stay inside because you haven't met targets this morning and I'm not particularly happy about your work, so you just sit there and think about it. In fact you can't have your lunch break either!" It's just absurd!

Kathy Brodie: I think that's so true. And if you say it with a lot of things if you say "would you treat an adult like that?" it'd be "Oh, no" but they are 'only' a child or they are a child which is like it is it's pretty appalling isn't it. So, although the children display the behaviour, the challenge comes from the fact that as adults *we* are challenged by that behaviour, rather than the behaviour itself being challenging. So that's kind of where we start with the challenging behaviour.

Where did the Phoenix Cups come from then where did they fit into this picture?

Sandi Phoenix: I was teaching about this for a long time about children's behaviour and I was getting less and less time with educators. There was a time where I had weeks and weeks with them to coach them and mentor them. And then as my career changed and evolved I was getting a couple of hours at a time. So I had to get really efficient at delivering the best bits of my message.

So way back in about 2002 I actually attended a presentation by Dr. Margaret Carter, who is well known here in Australia for her work as a psychologist. Her work introduced me to Choice Theory and the work of William Glasser and Dr. Glasser's work who I have come to know very well in and love very well over the many years since 2002.

Then a few years into my study of Glasser's work and study of psychology, I was teaching some educators in one of these short sessions about children's behaviour using an eclectic variety of theoretical frameworks. And I was talking a bit about this, a bit about that, about Glasser and it was all coming together in 'the children's behaviour is a function that is being driven by basic human life need'. So it has that function behind it. This is a need and the child is trying to meet this need with their behaviour was the gist of it. We had a really visual group in front of us trying to work out how to explain this. These water glasses were on the table I said "All right - this is the need for freedom; and this is the need for fun; and this is a need for power. And let's just imagine we've got to fill all those all day". And then I went "Oh. Gosh. That's brilliant. I. Am. A. Genius!" because at that point everybody just went, OK, I get it. OK.

I was talking theoretical frameworks and pedagogical approaches, I was freaking people out. I started talking about Cups – Right! I get Cups, they don't have the capacity to understand the psychobabble I was starting to go on with. Their brain was full, educators have so much going on. The last thing they need is 50 other theories that they have never heard about before. And so just to pull it all together and say 'there's five Cups - lets fill them' it just went from there. So the Cups framework was born and I was teaching it for many years.

People kept emailing me and saying "I can't find anything about the Cups". And I'd say - for the last time I've told you go and look at Maslow's work, Glassers work - they don't talk about Cups but you'll get it! So, by popular demand, we've actually developed a kit and a whole philosophy, we call it, in a framework for services to implement using the Cups philosophy.

Kathy Brodie: So tell me about the what the Cups names? Are they sort of specific areas, specific names?

Sandi Phoenix: They're certainly heavily based on Glassers Choice Theory. The training itself, actually is influenced by a few other theoretical frameworks and my own work. But the Cups are very similar to Glasser's work.

This is our mounted piece that hangs in the foyer. You can talk to parents about it so: * pointing to one cup at a time * that's Fun Cup, and then we have Power Cup, Freedom Cup, Love Cup, and Survival Cup. It's that basic - fill those Cups and we have happy children with a strong sense of well-being.

Kathy Brodie: And I can see, as you say, it's very visual you can see the Love Cup is empty then you've got a problem haven't you and.

Sandi Phoenix: See! And you haven't even done the training yet! It's ridiculously simple. We have an empty Love Cup - we all know what an empty Love Cup feels like - and we know what we need to fill it.

Kathy Brodie: So that's a really nice simple way, as you say, to have some really complex theories and psychology, that's been developed over decades centuries in some cases. But that's a really nice clear visual way of showing it. And I love the idea of hanging it in the hallway as well so you can share that with parents. I think that's so important isn't it, that home learning environment and taking that home as well.

Sandi Phoenix: Sometimes parents are so grateful, I end up doing the training for parents as well. So a lot of the time I come back in and do the training once a year with services because they've got new team members that are saying "what are these Cups that everyone's talking about?"

The other thing that used to happen is educators would email me and say "Can you tell me the name of the Cups again. Because we actually just now remember fun and freedom in that we forgot the rest". All that doesn't happen anymore because they've got that constant reminder.

Kathy Brodie: That's really useful as you say - there's so many other things going on. And I think that's the same for educators around the world. Constant pressure of more and more things having to do. Something really simple and visual, so beneficial for everybody.

Just thinking on a practical basis, because a lot of what I'd like at this Summit is these practical strategies that people can take away. How can educators impact issues apply some of those theories actually in their settings?

Sandi Phoenix: It's as simple as filling Cups. So the Cups kit and the training works you through step by step, how to develop a list of practical strategies around each Cup. But the general gist of that is - What can we do to fill Cups?

Reflect on a behavioural incidence - behavioural incidences and meltdowns and whatever challenging behaviour that you're having is actually your best research tool and learning tool. So take that as a blessing if you had a bad day because you're going to learn something out of there!

So let's reflect on:

What Cups were empty?

How did I contribute to that?

What did I do to empty Cups?

What did I do to fill Cups today?

What can I do tomorrow to make sure this Cup gets full, so I don't have a repeat of the same behaviour.

So, for example, I do know a lot of practitioners and I'm not sure how things look like there but certainly I would assume from colleagues I speak to it's much the same. Sometimes they make a decision to teach children in large groups. They bring children together in group time or circle time. And that time is often mandatory. So what we have during that time is a child who might be just not ready for that, particularly from a sensory perspective. He is still developing and integrating his senses and he needs to be outside.

So he or she will sit there fidgeting, rolling around on the floor, climbing over each other, making funny noises. And during that time the educator does all sorts of things to manage the child's behaviour. (And I also don't use that term, management either but that's a conversation for another day). But they'll have to manage that behaviour.

What happens during that group time or circle time, the child's Freedom Cup gets emptied, their Love Cup gets emptied, their Fun Cup gets emptied, the Power Cup emptied. Power, recognition, competence, control all goes in one Cup - emptied, thrown across the room.

So we get a child who reacts appropriately for when you have an empty Cup and he'll have a meltdown - yell and scream or call the teacher something that she may or may not have deserved. And then, it's meltdown time.

We can reflect on this and then ensure that during that time we're filling Cups. So get your children:

How can I fill my freedom Cup right before I'm about to do group time?

How can my decision to do group time respect the child's need to have a full power Cup or full freedom cup?

We can just make tiny little decisions during that time that are Cup *filling*. Or we could make minute changes and they're Cup *emptying*. So just being mindful to fill Cups. It is that easy!

I could give you five billion strategies, but you're going to come up with the best ones for you as soon as you start thinking along those lines.

Kathy Brodie: That was something I was going to pick up on that. I'm guessing it's going to be a different strategy for each child - each child's freedom Cup is going to be filled in a different way. As an educator and tuning into the children you're going to know that child, know what it is that really will fill that Cup for them.

That might be some really simple strategies you've got in place but sometimes it's just remembering that - just thinking about it. If it's giving them a five minute countdown or something. You need to remember to do that. Maybe just the Cup sat on the windowsill just triggers that memory doesn't it. Just that thought.

Sandi Phoenix: Yes absolutely. In the training we also find out how to understand the child's different needs profile. So actually we all have different size Cups. So I have some really massive Cup for power recognition, competence and control. It's huge. So thank goodness I'm the boss and I think that's why! I'm not, actually, I'm not really the boss because I hired someone to be the boss, she's way better at it. But I like to make all of the decisions, I like to be involved in everything, everywhere. It drives my partner crazy that I need to read an order off the menu and he can't because of my huge Power Cup.

We can identify with each other who have huge Power Cups we 'get' each other, we understand each other. I'm talking about my Cup so you can start to think about your own. But then I also have a really small, tiny, insy-winsy Survival Cup so I can have five hours sleep, come to work sick. And I don't need food for a while - I do need coffee though - Bit of coffee. I'm good to go.

Other people have a really big Survival Cup and they need lots of sleep. So when we start to understand our own needs profiles then we can start to understand the children's needs profiles. To think more along the lines of needs profiles, I'd highly recommend Dr. William Glasser's book on Choice Theory and of course any of his work.

As far as the Cups go and practical strategies around working in education and care, we get all that out in the training. It's really fun to think about and to get to know your own needs profile.

Then, as soon as you start to understand the child whose challenging you, their needs profile, you go "Ah he's got a huge Power Cup like me. No wonder we're having issues with each other because when I'm filling mine, I'm emptying his out and when he is trying to fill his, I'm emptying his out". I'm like "No, don't take my power". When we understand each other's profiles like that, it just gets a whole lot easier.

Kathy Brodie: I'm guessing there, children change during the time they are with us, even during the day possibly? That those Cups will change size. There will be occasions where they'll need different sorts of things. Although we talk about children's needs, thinking about it in that physical way and saying - actually we need to expand his love Cup absolutely massively because he's got this going on at home more and more and having to fill.

Sandi Phoenix: Yes. And what I explain in this training is that if we think of the actual size of the Cups is quite static. They stay the same, most of the time throughout our lifespan, but their varying levels of full and empty.

So you might have a really big Power Cup. But today it's full because you got to do all this stuff with grandma and grandpa on the weekend and they gave him lots of power and control over everything. And then he's come to Kindi this morning and it's actually quite full. Or he's had the opposite and he's had a weekend where he's had no involvement in the decision making process about when he goes. He was whipped into Dads and then Mum came and picked him up early, because Mum and Dad had a fight and they're not together. He's got no power and no control over his situation at all. And then he walks into Kindi and he knows this is the place where I fill my Power Cup up - "right, all of you guys, *you're* going to fill my Power Cup up today".

So when we're sensitive to whether or not it's full or empty we start to have a little more compassion and the behaviour becomes less challenging to us and more about what can I do here. As an educator, what decisions can I make to fill these Cups? It empowers you, because you realise that you actually can do something about it once you understand.

Kathy Brodie: I think that's one of the things I really liked about it, it's a very positive message. You're not talking about the negativity, it's very positive. What can we do to help? Rather than what do we do to manage or squash that behaviour.

So there's lots and lots of things we've covered there already but what would your top tip be for any practitioners or educators listening today?

Sandi Phoenix: Probably feel the Love Cup first. So your connect, your relationship is a priority. Children really can't learn from outside of a healthy relationship of love and trust.

If you want a child to learn from you, and I'm speaking about behavioural learning, then you need to have the relationship with the child first. If you don't have a relationship with the child, don't attempt to manage their behaviour. They're not going to learn from you. Just connect with them, build your relationship, fill their love Cup in any way that you can work out how. Then work on what we can do. Because once you have a connection with a child you can see their needs profile better.

Before we truly connect with them you can't say what Cups are big and small and what Cups are full and empty so connected attunement and then go from there.

Kathy Brodie: That's super advice and that that connection I think is so basic it's fundamental. I think it's a fundamental human right, isn't it really that you should have some way to connect like that. That's absolutely amazing. Have you got some of your resources with you that we could have a look at?

Sandi Phoenix: Yes I do and I'm super proud of our Cups. I'll just show you. They come in this cute little bag with all the Cups on it. It's pretty gorgeous. And then we got some reflection cards, so just when you want to have a super brainstorming session around the Cups, which have questions on them, that's pretty cool.

And there is a workbook that works you through everything that we talk about in the training. And also we have a three part series webinar that comes with the Cups kit. So you buy the Cups kit and then you do the three part series training, which we run every quarter, every three or four months. And then last but not least we have a white board posters. So put these in the staff room or wherever you're going to collaborate together with a colleague. You write Cups filling strategies that really worked for you today with our Phoenix support whiteboard marker.

And I say these are just beautiful. They were designed by an artist and friend of mine Melissa Underwood from the Creativity Canvas. So she has done a great job with these.

And then there's all you posters for your Cup filling strategies and we write on them to keep it really visual and keep us thinking about the practical strategies that we're using. And of course there's the what we call the bathroom poster because we often find these motivational posters go in the bathroom or on the toilet door around here. So this poster says "You can't pour from an empty Cup. How do you fill yours?" Really thinking about your own Cups now.

Kathy Brodie: it's quite important as well isn't it, you recognising your own Cups but you make sure that yours are full and adequate as well. Would you expect to refresh those every day is that a constant reflective tool?

Sandi Phoenix: They're particularly good for staff meetings or sitting with a colleague, if you don't have a whole staff team, and discussing things and getting them down. Putting them up visually and then just adding to them or changing them as you go.

Keep them as dynamic as you need to for a while. And then after you've used them for a while you might want to wipe them all off and just let them sit there as an art piece and then come back to it in a couple of weeks, when you need reminding. Because sometimes we slip back into some old ways and then we need to go back – "What was that framework we were using? what's that philosophy? It was really working". I do find though that people who've done their Cups training rarely lose that because it is such a concrete thinking.

When we do the training, we go right through stories. We talk about Jayden and Sally - two children and their different stories - and when we start to visualize together, that visualization helps us to remember the analogy and the theory for a really long time. So I do find that educators rarely slip back to completely old ways but sometimes we need reminding to get back into what are those practical strategies I need to try.

Kathy Brodie: I think that's really good practice anyway just to reflect constantly and just remind yourself that the children have grown a bit. You've got a new cohort. You know all these things and we might have had life experiences have changed us as well so that it's a reflection I think is very good practice anyway.

I think that's a great idea. That has just been amazing. I'm so pleased that you were able to come onto the Summit and tell us all about Phoenix Cups. I just think the pictures are gorgeous. I've not seen those resources before I think they're beautiful. And I would love them as art work. They're just really nice.

So how did you find out about more about the Phoenix Cups and about yourself and the work that you do. Where would they go to.

Sandi Phoenix: Best place is our website: www.phoenix-support.com.au. There's resources for educators section there and in that section is an order form for the Cups kit.

Also our blog post. You might have picked up that I'm a little opinionated and quite free flowing with that opinion. So that goes on in the blog posts. There is certainly one that is relevant to this conversation about filling the freedom Cup on there It's called The Advocate for Childhood.

So there's plenty of different ways on our website and of course we have a Facebook page and Instagram and all connected through there. But please do friend me on Facebook because I like friends I'm Sandi Phoenix.

Kathy Brodie: Thank you so much Sandi and the links are on the Summit website so you can click through next to the video and you'll be able to go straight onto those websites and Facebook page. So that's would really good if you can do that. And Sandi thank you so much for joining us today from Australia, it has been an absolute honour and pleasure to talk with you today. And thank you for sharing your resources with us. It's been absolutely fascinating.

Sandi Phoenix: Thank you so much for inviting me. And I'll speak to you soon.

CHAPTER 9

PSED AND CHILDREN WITH AUTISM

Michelle Myers

Kathy Brodie: I am very excited to be joined by a long time personal friend of mine, Michelle Myers also known as Mrs M when she writes on my blog. She's a writer and blogger, but first and foremost a busy mum of three.

She's a carer for her autistic son but has also worked for over 15 years in childcare and education as a nursery manager then as a higher level teaching assistant. She went on to specialize in supporting children with autism in primary schools as well as providing training support for teachers and other learning support staff.

She started writing her blog as a way of sharing her story and raising awareness, which has led to a Facebook support page for others professionals and for parents as well. It's called 'A Slice of Autism' and you find that link there next to us on the on the website right now. I'm absolutely thrilled to be joined by Michelle. Welcome to the summit.

Michelle Myers: Thanks Kathy. Thanks for having me.

Kathy Brodie: It's a real pleasure. It's lovely to see you here today. We're going to be looking at personal, social and emotional development, but particularly for children on the autistic spectrum because that's your area specialism and you've seen it both as a parent and in nursery and in schools. So I just want to draw on that wealth of experience that you have.

Before we go on to personal, social and emotional development though, I know your blog is really, really popular. I just want to have a little brief chat about how that came about and what it is that you get from writing the blog.

Michelle Myers: Well, I was working full time in mainstream school up to about two years ago. And I was going to work every day and speaking to my friends about funny situations that would happen at home. They would always say to me "you should write this down, you know you should share this, you should. It's an insight into your world really".

For instance, the time that my son decided that he wanted to dry himself. So he tried to climb in the dryer, because that's where things get dry!

I'd go in and talk about these stories and we weren't laughing *at* him, but it was just a way for me to offload. And often the stories would end up being quite amusing, because he did get up to some stuff when he was younger. On one occasion, we needed to buy new coat for him. So we went to Marks and Spencer's and he is very specific about the sounds of textures and things. So he proceeded to try this coat on but wanted to know how noisy it was. So he rolled around the floor in the middle of Marks and Spencer. As you can imagine, we got some funny looks!

You know this is the kind of thing I would go in and talk to my friends and colleagues about. It wasn't until my situation at home changed quite drastically and he wasn't coping in school. I had to give my job up, because I had to part home-school him. He was only managing about two hours a day in school at this point. So I hit rock bottom really. My mental health deteriorated quite significantly and it was hard.

I remember feeling quite lonely and quite isolated and feeling I was the only person going through this. So that's when I thought "you know what, why not give it a go?" So I started writing down things that happened, just as a way of me processing what was going on to start with. That's when a few people got wind of the fact that I was writing. I was brave enough to press publish and put it out there and to sort of never really look back from then.

I just know how scared I felt. I wasn't sure how honest I could be in my writing, because that's quite scary. There have been many times when I've written, I've been really scared to press publish because I'd been quite open and quite honest and 'warts and all' - it's kind of a phrase that I came up with - but I just felt I had to be. If I was going to do it then I had to do it properly and let people know what life was really like. So that was kind of where it started.

Kathy Brodie: So I can understand that met a need for you, but you've gone on to write for The Mighty, Special Needs Jungle, Autism parent, SEN magazines - all massive publications and anybody who's dealt with special education needs will be aware of all those publications. So they've gone out to a big audience. What sort of response have you had from them?

Michelle Myers: Bonkers, really! I really had no idea at the time quite what response I would get. I don't know if anybody would read anything I was writing but it took me by surprise.

I think part of the appeal is that people can see... I think if you're writing about authentic experiences and being really honest and saying "look, this is me" I think people can really pick up on that. I think they can sense if I'm sort of holding back.

I always try and write about things that are brutally honest, no matter how scary that is. I mean some of the blogs seem to have had a life of their own really, and that's been something I've had to learn to accept. You have to let them go. Some of the blogs, particularly the one I wrote for you about autism and the Delayed Effect, just went crazy. And I have to stop reading the comments because, although there were so many positive comments, it's quite hard to read some of the things that people say. So that was sort of a process that I've had to learn to let go of some of the blogs. But I have been blown away about is that the hundreds of people have contacted me to say that I've written things that made them cry. That they've read something I've written and it's like I was telling their story. And you know it's affected them to the point that they felt they needed to contact me and say that. I can't tell you how humbling that is. There's nothing more powerful than that.

I think that's the reason why I'm going to keep on doing what I'm doing because it's important that people know. Mums I think particularly, it can be very isolating and very confusing particularly if they're waiting so long for a diagnosis.

It took my son almost five years getting a diagnosis and it's so difficult because you can't access services. You are judged as a parent everything you do seems scrutinized. School don't always understand. It's so difficult. And I do what I do, to let people know that they're not alone in feeling like that and that there is light at the end of the tunnel. You know things do get better. There are dark days. Things do get better. So over and above that, I think that's kind of why I'm going to keep doing what I do.

Kathy Brodie: Absolutely and I know that it does help people. I've certainly had people email me and say "This is fantastic. I've not been able to explain to school, so I've printed it off to take it and I've shown the teacher" and that's a really nice way of supporting people as well.

Michelle Myers: It's scary really, if I think about it too much, but I can't let that stop me writing I've just got to carry on like this.

Kathy Brodie: Absolutely! Moving on to the focus of the Summit. We're looking at personal, social and emotional development. Obviously every child is unique but all children develop in slightly different ways. They will have their own little things, but no more so than children on the autistic spectrum, which is obviously why it's called a spectrum. But first of all, could you just give us a little bit of an overview of what you might expect from your child on the autistic spectrum and also the challenges that they might have with personal, social and emotional development.

Michelle Myers: So I have to admit, Kathy, that when I found out what the topic of the Summit was I felt a bit overwhelmed. I mean, where do I even begin? Because at its very core, autism is a condition that affects how people see the world and how they interact, how they communicate. So I felt a bit like "Eeeek" where do I begin, it's so huge.

But if you look at the Early Years Foundation Stage (EYFS), personal, social and emotional development is recognized as the building blocks to success in life. It enables children to interact with others and have growing positive attitudes towards themselves and other people. But obviously it needs adults and other children to model appropriate behaviour for them to be able to develop.

If we look at what the National Autistic Society says about autism it states that autism is *'a lifelong developmental disability that affects how a person communicates with and relates to other people and have experience the world around them'*. So one of the core deficits of autism is communicating and interacting with the world around them.

So, how can we navigate through all the stages of personal, social and emotional development with children that may never meet all those statements or those building blocks of development? Some of them may meet some and not others.

Obviously, each child is different and develops at their own pace. But I think no more can this be seen than with children with autism. It's a spectrum for a reason, because they are all so different. When I worked in a mainstream primary I worked in a resourced provision and we had eight or nine children, I think, across the school, every single one of them was different. Every one of them hit different milestones had different needs. Yes, they all have that diagnosis of autism. But within that diagnosis were so many different needs and it was our job to cater for all those individual needs.

The developmental path that children on the spectrum can take, can look very, very different from children who are not on the autistic spectrum. It got me thinking - who's to say that that's wrong? Really it's not. It's just a different way of looking at it, because children see the world in a completely different way to the way that we do.

I think it's our job as professionals to find a way of bridging the gap between the two worlds. It's not a case of forcing them into our world. Its a case of us finding strategies and finding ways to get into their world to bridge that gap, to open lines of communication for them. But I have to say it's not easy, working with children on the autism spectrum - hats off to anybody that does it in a mainstream school. I know it's hard, it's hard work. It's extremely rewarding when you get it right.

But it can be very, very hard work because lots of children with autism can have difficulties right across all aspects of daily life. What we used to find was that they would have spiky profiles, so, they would meet some targets, really struggle with some particular areas of personal, social and emotional development and yet be flying away in maths. So you would have these very sort of spiky profile children.

What I thought I would do is look at the various sorts of areas of personal, social and emotional development because it's such a huge area for children with autism and maybe just focus in on a couple of specific subject areas of difficulty.

I thought we'd look first at making relationships. For lots of children they can have difficulty processing information. They can be quite rigid and quite inflexible with their thoughts and thinking and can take things that people say quite literally. And that can get them in all sorts of trouble in social situations because they can misunderstand what is being said. They can take something literally. I remember once telling a child go back down the corridor and wash your hands and walked backwards down the corridor! That completely makes sense because that's what I said to him.

So you do have to be very careful about the sort of language that you use with children. They can also need a longer time to process information, which can make two way conversations quite difficult, quite challenging for them because they simply can't keep up with what's being said. They can't keep up with the pace of the language. And this can make it quite hard to make friendships because sometimes it just become all a bit too complicated. So it's easier to withdraw themselves than to put themselves in the centre of it all because it can just become overwhelming for them really.

Lots of children on the autism spectrum have poor executive functioning skills, which can mean that they can struggle to pay attention, struggle to plan and organize themselves and recognize and follow what's happening in class. You will often see children with autism a couple of steps behind, following. Teachers can assume they must be keeping up because - look everyone's lined up and there he is, he's lined up. But often, if you look really carefully and just take a step back and watch what's going on, you'll see that often they are just a few steps behind everybody else, so they're taking their visual cues from what everybody else is doing. It's not necessarily knowing that this is what we're meant to do.

That's a case of observing and taking the time. It's really, really important to don't throw yourself in there. Just sit back take your time and observe. I learned so much from observing the children. And looking really, really carefully at the kind of things they do. It does tell you so much. I think very easily we can make assumptions when with children.

Another thing that they can struggle with is that they can have difficulty controlling their emotions and their behaviours. Children can often act on impulse because they can't always forward think what the consequences of their actions might be. And for some children it can be a constant battle to match their behaviour to the certain demands that are required of them. For many children that's a constant battle, particularly in new and unfamiliar situations because it involves so much multitasking and forward thinking that it can be very challenging for them.

Children on the autism spectrum can find it quite hard sometimes to see the grey areas particularly in social situations. So there can often be a right answer and a wrong answer but never an in between, not many grey areas. If we think about that in the context of social situations, it can make it really hard for them to participate because there are so many hidden nuances and rules, complex interactions - when should I speak?

There's so many hidden rules! You speak to certain people some ways, you don't approach the head teacher in that way. Lots of these are assumptions, we assume that people know and children pick up on it. But the children on the autism spectrum can't always see those hidden rules. And so it's our job to clarify those things for them and navigate these social situations for them.

Often they can find themselves in conflicts with other children because they have no room for compromise. It's their way or no way. And they can struggle with that interaction that occurs every day amongst peers in the nursery and in the classroom because they're so rigid in their thinking and they can't always see things from the other person's point of view.

Having conversations can be really, really difficult for children on the autism spectrum because, if you think about it, it involves so many different skills. We take it for granted and assume, but we forget that so much processing is going on behind the scenes. And for children on the autism spectrum it can be really, really difficult to filter out all these things:

read people's facial expressions

maintain eye contact, which can be very difficult for them

use of gesture. For some children on the autism spectrum you would wave at them and they wouldn't even know what that was.

reading people's body language

understanding the other person's point of view

gauging the response

thinking what to say next so that kind of forward thinking and forward planning

That sort of quick fire to and fro of communication can be really, really tricky. We pick up on so much that children on the autism spectrum can find really difficult.

For instance, I think you've possibly built up a picture of who I am, because so much is going on subconsciously, you're making judgments all the time. Either the way people act or how people sound. That could be a really difficult element of the day for children, they can find it really hard.

As a result of these difficulties children can find themselves getting into trouble at school, particularly I'm thinking of children who don't necessarily have that diagnosis. In a way a diagnosis is tricky really because – yes, it's putting a label on a child but what it also offers a level of protection in some ways. It makes people a little bit more understanding, I think, if you've got a child that people are struggling with in school, there's issues and he hasn't got a diagnosis. It can be very tricky for them to do to navigate their way through school. So it really is vital that children get diagnosed as early as possible. But that's a whole other story isn't it really.

So, I was thinking about the playground for children. This was an area that we had to really staff quite heavily at school because if there was ever going to be an issue it was going to be in the playground. You've got all the sensory issues going on in the playground (which is a whole other thing) and all this social interaction.

What we used to find often was children having a game of tag or something. And naturally the game evolves and flows and the rules change. It could be, now the logs the base or now you're 'it' or somebody could say I don't want to play anymore. For the children on the spectrum that can be really difficult because they've got comfortable with the rules of the game playing in a certain way and then all of a sudden everyone shouting "Oh now the logs are the base" - Well, hang on a minute, the logs weren't the base a minute ago!

The potential for difficulty in those kind of situations is quite large really. So we had to staff play time with three or four members of staff to be dealing with all the issues that would be going on in the playground. So what you will often find is that lots of children can find themselves getting in trouble at play time. What they will do to compensate is trying take over the game or become quite bossy and these quickly escalates and they can lash out.

There's issues for lining up at playtime. Some of them might want to be at the front of the line or they don't like people touching them. So playtimes can be a particularly difficult part of the day for children.

Sadly it can mean that children get labelled as 'naughty'. I know we shouldn't use that kind of word really - it is not something we ever did - but amongst the children I think its very easy for the child with autism who has difficulties at playtime to become that child that other kids don't want to play with.

You have to work very, very hard to scaffold those times, those three play times are really difficult for children on the spectrum, so anything that we can do - it could be setting up a quiet area of the playground where they can go and take maybe one or two friends to go and play with themselves so that they're still having that interaction but doing something that's not setting them up to fail.

What we used to do with some children is have a buddy system so we would pair up some younger children with an older child. They loved that. The older children taking responsibility of a younger child it was classed as a badge of honour.

Another thing we used to do was we used to train the lunch staff and we used to give them resources and little booklets with visuals that they could take with simple playground games where the rules are consistent. And again it's adult led so it's all being modelled and they can keep an eye on what's going on.

So there's lots of things that can be done. You know it's hard. You don't get time to go to the loo. You need a coffee. And you're so busy supporting them in the classroom that you think "right know they're outside just going to nip to the toilet really quickly". But in actual fact they're probably the times that the children need more support, not less. What we tend to do is reduce support at those times and then we end up coming out the toilet with kids screaming saying "such and such has just hit me", you know that kind of thing.

It could be a case of you go out at play times to support them at play time and then you can set them up at a quiet task and then nip to the loo or something like that. It's a case of managing your time and seeing play time as a priority, which I think it does need to be.

It can be difficult for children on the spectrum to understand how their friends can be feeling. Seeing things from the other person's point of view, understanding why they're upset, could be difficult for them. And so this can make building close friendships for children really challenging and they can't always see how their actions can impact on how other children feel about them. You know, they might get really upset in a game, have a meltdown and lash out and then 10 minutes later not quite understand why the child that got caught in the thrashing is upset with them.

So it's very important that you know once things have calmed down we revisit those situations and use them as a learning tool. You could use models, books and props. There's all sorts of different things that you could use but don't try and do it in the heat of the moment. It's very important that you wait because it can take a long time. Physically on the outside they might appear as if everything's fine and everything's back to normal. But inside they've probably got all these emotions going on and it is important that we give them time and then we go back and reflect on it. So look at what happened, try and get them to see from the other person's point of view. Then, at that point, put a strategy in place. So if this happens again, you know what you can you do. For example, you could use your visuals, so that's the time to do that, not in the heat of the moment where everything is happening

Another area of personal, social and emotional development is self-confidence and self awareness. Now, when I was thinking about this I think this is quite a biggie really. Well, they're all big issues, overwhelming I think.

For my son particularly, I think he's got used to living in a world where he doesn't quite fit in, particularly when he was in mainstream primary. He was the child that was struggling. He was the child that was pacing up and down the back of the classroom with everyone turning around and going "Why is he doing that?" Things got so bad for him that he was self harming in school. I can't even begin to imagine how it must have felt for him, living in a world that I think people didn't understand him. He was a 'problem'. He was he was a burden and he didn't fit in with everybody. And I think he was ... Well like I said I can't even begin to imagine how having must've felt.

It affected his mental health really, really severely. I've been out with Owen and people stare. People can be rude, people can be judgmental and it's hard for me BUT I have to stop and think to myself - if it's hard for me how hard must it be for him. How must HE feel?

You imagine living in a world that's actually really inflexible. You know, we sort of say children with autism are inflexible, they're rigid, they don't see things from other people's point of view. I think we're just as guilty of that. We make judgments. We can't necessarily always see it from their point of view. We try to put labels on things to explain it.

And I think often people can see autism as something that can be treated. Again that's a whole other story, but imagine living with that feeling that YOU were a problem, you were a burden, you had something that could be cured, could be taken away from you. You could be made to look 'less autistic'. Imagine what that must do to children.

The signs of autism like hand flapping and stimming. Some people think they're bad and try and stop them. Force eye contact. I can't think of any other disability that can be treated (not everybody does) but can be treated in such a way. And I can't imagine how that would feel.

It made me think of the book - I don't know if you've ever read it - The Reason I Jump. Have you ever read it?

Kathy Brodie: Oh yes.

Michelle Myers: It's an amazing book and it made me think of something that Naoke [the author] said. So I just wanted to read it to you. So somebody said to him "What's the worst thing about having autism?" And he said "you never really notice. Really. You have no idea quite how miserable we are. The people who were looking after us say - minding these kids is really hard work for you. But for us, who are always causing the problems and are useless at pretty much everything we do you can't begin to imagine how miserable and sad we get".

Kathy Brodie: Wow, that is so powerful. This a book that was written by a Japanese dad interviewing his son with autism and spoke to him and asked him those questions

Michelle Myers: Well he was nonverbal, this little boy, but they managed to find a communication device for him. If you haven't read it, I'd highly recommend reading this book because it really makes you think about us seeing things from the child's point of view. It's definitely worth a read.

My son was living in a world at this point, going back about three years ago, where he didn't fit. His mental health deteriorated so quickly. And I think that's something that we need to be very cautious of when we're working with children with autism. It can be very tempting to try and force them into our world, to try to say this is a problem behaviour. What can we do to stop them doing this behaviour? But I think we need to just take a step back and think OK, well is this behaviour serving a purpose? It most probably is. If you speak to any adult with autism they will say that stimming is something they need to do.

Kathy Brodie: Stimming is that hand flapping, for example.

Michelle Myers: It can be a variety of things. For some people it's hand flapping, for some people it's spinning. My son paces when he is anxious. He will pace around and around and around and around. And that's what he needs to do in order to sort of get himself back to where he needs to be. Okay it might look a little bit strange but is he doing anybody any harm?

It's often a way that children have found themselves, to keep themselves regulated. It's how they cope with being in our world. And I think, particularly thinking about self-awareness, do we want these children to be in an environment where they feel out of sync with everybody else, where their stimming is seen as something that should be stopped? Put your hands down or that kind of thing.

I think it's something that we just need to have in the forefront of our minds all the time. In particular reference to this area because anxiety as well is so huge for children with autism. If you have heard of the round peg square hole thing. You know we're sort of chipping away at them effectively. I remember hearing a really great analogy which was a ruler and you know you can bend and bend and bend on bend a ruler so much that at some point it's going to snap. You can bend it up to a certain point and it's going to snap and that's what life can be like for the children.

I think that's what happened with my son, he just got to a point where he'd snapped and everything around him just collapsed. He went into an acute period of clinical anxiety, was self harming, was school refusing and this can be so hard for parents.

So many times I've heard teachers say "They can't get him here in the morning. They just need to be a bit firmer with them". No! You have no idea! I mean there were some days I used to drop Owen off at school and I would have spent two and a half hours of him in complete panic about the day ahead. I bought one of these (shakes can of soda) – it's that shaking of the can thing, isn't it.

I would sit in my car in the morning, after dropping him off and I would just be exhausted – physically, mentally, emotionally exhausted. It has an impact on the whole family.

I think another key point maybe is to really listen to the parents. If they're coming in and saying to you "look, you're telling me he's fine at school but this is what we're having at home". Please believe them! Please believe the parents, they don't want to come in and have these conversations with you! We would love to just be able to pick our children up at the end of the day and everything be fine. "How is your day son? Oh yeah, it was great". That would be lovely, you know. We're not attention seekers.

We don't say this because we want to come into school and speak to you. We're saying this because we've reached the end of our tether, because we're exhausted.

I think it's important that we treat parents with that level of respect because they're professionals in their own children. They know their children inside-out and it can very quickly escalate to become a real mental health problem. And we all know again, that's another issue, but mental health services in this country are not the best at all are they? So all we can do to avoid children needing access to those services, the better really.

I think a big part of that is that these kids need to know that they're valued. They need to know that we respect who they are. They need to know that – yes, their autism is a part of who they are - but they're amazing just like every other child that comes into the classroom. They're not a problem. They don't have challenging behaviour that we have to stamp out. It's part of who they are. And I think it's our job to you know to unpick those issues and see that actually, that they have a lot to offer the world. So that was my feeling with self-confidence.

Kathy Brodie: We've covered an awful lot. There's been lots of practical advice, lots of things to be thinking about. And obviously I think that's really interesting about the label. Until you get that label and get that diagnosis it is very difficult then to apply for some of those things.

So you've already given us a few ideas on supporting children in some of those areas. But what would your top tip be? What would be the one thing that you would like practitioners, teachers, parents possibly to go away and think about when thinking about children on the autistic spectrum.

Michelle Myers: Oh gosh top tips! I think probably my take home message would be that, if we always assume that children are doing the best in any given situation, then that puts the emphasis on us, as the educators to analyse in what's going on.

So don't assume that we have all the answers, because we don't. And they can teach us as much as we can teach them, if we let them. Their autism might prevent them from ticking all those boxes in your assessments. But I think we can very easily become bogged down on what children CAN'T do.

It's vital that we start where they're at and build on that, rather than focussing on everything that they can't do. Well what can they do? And how can we extend that? How can we use their special interests to slowly, slowly, slowly kind of push and build, rather than - they can't do that, so we're going to give up on it. Because they have as much rights as every child that walks through that door in the morning to a full, inclusive education and if that means that we have to think outside the box a little bit then I think that that's what we need to be doing.

I think we have to just remember that it's just a different way of seeing the world. It's not wrong. It is different. It can be technicolour and glorious, it can be confusing and really, really mysterious but it's never wrong. It's never inferior. It's just wonderfully different. So that would be my key message really.

Kathy Brodie: Absolutely. That ties in with a lot of your other messages there with standing back and taking a minute, working out what is actually happening. When children are stimming, what they're going through, what it is that they do, why they do that to meet needs. Do we need to stop it?

Now I know that you have a book 'A Slice of Autism' and I love the subtitle which is 'What's normal anyway?' And I think that's exactly sums up a lot of what we've covered here today. You can find the link there to the site of autism book and you can buy that off Amazon or any other good bookshop. You'll find the link there to the blogspot which is also 'A Slice of Autism'. And I know that you update that regularly. There's loads of really great resources on there.

I will warn you now, you will have to sit down when you read it because very often I see it, then and weep a few tears and then have to have a reflective think on that. So it is it's a really warts and all as you say. It's a really honest blogspot which is great. And as you say that's exactly what parents need they need that support as well.

Michelle, we could just sit and talk all day. Thank you so so much for sharing your expertise with us on the Early Years Web Summit.

Michelle Myers: Thank you. Thanks for having me.

Kathy Brodie: Oh it's been a real pleasure.

CHAPTER 10

PEDAGOGICAL DOCUMENTATION

Debi Keyte-Hartland

Kathy Brodie: I'm delighted to be joined by Debi Keyte-Hartland. Debi is an international freelance consultant and blogger who explores approaches of education that creates fertile conditions for deep thinking of both children and educators. She's an advocate for the use of the visual arts as a tool for creative and critical thinking and how the expressive languages can embrace values for active listening and documentation and the co-construction of knowledge is part of a group. She's co-director of sightlines initiative. Welcome to the Early Years Web Summit, Debi.

Debi Keyte-Hartland: Thank you. Thank you so much for us to be part of this wonderful opportunity.

Kathy Brodie: I couldn't miss this, because we will be talking about documentation today and how that can support children's personal, social and emotional development. And I have to admit at this point, when we talk about documentation, I think about this as being 'the boring paperwork' part. Nobody wants to talk about documentation.

You're specifically talking about pedagogical documentation. So I was fascinated to find out what that was about. Could you just start with: what is pedagogical documentation, please?

Debi Keyte-Hartland: Well for me, it's not the boring stuff but it's the essential stuff of trying to figure out the process of how children are learning and developing.

So it's trying to get to the bigger picture of what our children are thinking about. And I suppose it's a research methodology in that it has both a form and a function. So for me, the form of pedagogical documentation takes the form of taking photographs which we'd ordinarily do within an Early Years setting, maybe taking some film and writing down some notes about what children say and do.

Then the functional side of it is in using that, rather than putting it in a book that goes on a shelf somewhere, for somebody to look at some point. We use those traces for self reflection, and for group reflection with others, and for sharing back with families and most importantly sharing back with the child. We use it so that we can we can figure out what to do next with children and trying to figure out what they are thinking about, so that our choices are better than before.

Kathy Brodie: So that sounds like it's very much a working document it is a process rather than just gathering dust somewhere.

Debi Keyte-Hartland: That's right, it's absolutely a process and I think sometimes documentation is a product. That it is something that the staff word process, the photographs added into, it goes on the wall or it goes in the children's file somewhere and it's quite a static product. Pedagogical documentation is very much a process that's alive and keeps the learning alive.

Kathy Brodie: And that's interesting point, because I see lots of documentation that is word processed, that's beautifully presented. I mean looks absolutely gorgeous, you can't knock that, but very often that's taken somebody's whole weekend to do that and it's not added much value to the children, but you're talking about something that's being used every day, is that right?

Debi Keyte-Hartland: Yeah that's right. I think the minute you pick up your camera, you are making a choice about something you are valuing, something that's happening. In that moment, you're picking up the camera, you begin to document. So it begins at that point, not at the point of putting things together in a nice package. We could call that more summative documentation, something that we might do at the end to share to a wider audience. But it's not the main thing that we do.

Kathy Brodie: How interesting. Pedagogical documentation's very much a working document it's something that's a process. So how can we use that to support children's personal social emotional development?

Debi Keyte-Hartland: You know, in collecting the traces of documentation of children's experiences, we can use these as visual aids and as memoirs to recreate a context for learning. The most important thing to do, is to be able to offer these traces, that we collect, back with the children.

Sometimes that's as easy as just turning the camera around or turning the tablet around so that they can see themselves. I think it's about seeing that children see themselves as learners and see the pleasure in that. They can reflect back on something. I often say to practitioners that what we've done is make external an experience that's internal for the children. They're feeling themselves as learners, as confident communicators. But then we're showing back to them, what that actually looks like and that gives more energy to the process of learning. And it also shows in terms of what we value - how we value children. You know it's so important that they have this sense of what they've got to say is important that the world and I've got something to offer the world. And pedagogical documentation, to me, does exactly that.

Kathy Brodie: I think there's an amount of respect comes in there as well, when you're talking about showing children what they have done. We are very quick to take photos and nobody actually says the child "Do you mind if I take a photo of your beautiful model here?" I love the idea. It is as simple as turning the camera around and just showing "look, what I've taken a photo of here".

Debi Keyte-Hartland: That starts the conversation and you find out more and it means you are in connection with that child. Then you're not viewing them through a lens all of the time - it's about forming a relationship with the child or the group of children that you are with.

Kathy Brodie: That's what lots of people say about documentation. The paperwork takes me away from the children, I want to be with the children, I came into the job to be with the children. I absolutely totally get that point of view and I absolutely agree with it. So maybe this is a way of both doing the documentation *and* being with the children, having that joint learning process together with them.

So it doesn't feel like you're being taken away by that documentation. What sort of things can practitioners be doing with pedagogical documentation? What sort of things does that encompass?

Debi Keyte-Hartland: Well, an example I can give you is with some educators at Ashmore Park Nursery in Wolverhampton, who use pedagogical documentation as part of their everyday practice.

Currently they've got some groups of children who are interested in the sun and the moon and the relationship between them. So a typical way of working with pedagogical documentation is that they would just keep a book by their sides. Just a simple notebook. And as they're working with the children and asking questions and watching and noticing what children are doing within that enquiry context they'll be jotting down what children say. And also, importantly, what children do but it's jotting down a sort of a personal memoir and that might also be writing down things that the children say.

They might have a particular question in mind that they want to document further, which might be about children's relationships or it might be about the relationship between the sun and the moon and what they're thinking about. So they're writing notes and interacting with the children at the same time. But the important thing is what they do then afterwards.

This book isn't just closed and then put on the shelf until the next time to add more notes into it. Neither is it used as a checklist to check off points against various criteria, but it's actually used in conversation and dialogue with each other as a place of exchange and encounter. They talk to each other about what's gone on and then ask each other "What do you think is happening within this?" They may then choose certain photographs that they've taken and bring them back to a group meeting.

You'll use those photographs that they have chosen in the next session when they're next with the group of children and say "This is what we were doing last time. Do you remember?" That gets the children talking back about what they're doing And sees them in that context of being creative and active learners.

Kathy Brodie: That's got so many valuable points. Very rarely - I'm just trying to think now - I don't think I've ever gone back to a group of children, got out of the book and said "Do you remember what we did last time?" and keeping children in mind and valuing their views. That's there, isn't it. That's all done for you. And how interesting having seen that in action. How do children respond to that. Are they quite positive?

Debi Keyte-Hartland: They're very positive about it!

In another context Madeley Nursery School, they have these reflections journals and they place them down on the floor and they've often got photographs that children have taken side by side with what they what they have said. And you'll often find that the children will try to add their own marks into it because they know that book is about them. They know that they can go back and find previous encounters that they've had together and they remember about that. What happens is that they begin to see themselves (of course they see themselves as an individual) as an individual, as part of a group, as part of a collective group. And it creates that sense of belonging that you want in a group of people, let alone children.

Kathy Brodie: I can imagine that might work really well with your key group as well. If you have a small group time with you a key group to get those sorts of things out and remind and reflect on what you've got there.

Debi Keyte-Hartland: I often say get the book out, so we can write it down.

Kathy Brodie: These are just normal books you're talking about. They're just A4 books of some sort?

Debi Keyte-Hartland: An A3 or A4 plain notebook. And sometimes you might want to draw how children have been drawing. For example you know the kinds of marks they're making. It is sort of a visual reminder that might be important at the time to look at. Or it might be that you want to draw where the children are positioned around a piece of paper if they're doing something collaborative.

Kathy Brodie: Those are reasonably simple things to do. It's almost like a change of attitude like a change of perspective on what it is that you're doing. We're not talking about really expensive pieces of kit here. But this is how you use everyday things that I'm sure people have already got in their settings.

Debi Keyte-Hartland: The first time I encountered pedagogical documentation was of course in the schools in Reggio Emilia in Italy and I was expecting to see something that was very complex, very complicated, very time consuming.

They showed us a video of some A3 photographs of children, black and white, simple, beautiful photographs of children, that were just laid out in the infant/toddler centres for their very young children. The babies would crawl up to these photographs. It's a very early form of documentation and they would encounter themselves. They would put their hands up against the images, they would look at each and they would go along the row, they would look at each others. That's pedagogical documentation being used in its simplest form to offer back to the children so that they can continue to construct an image of identity for themselves. It was a beautiful example of how simple documentation can be used back with the children.

Kathy Brodie: Again the practitioners are the educators. They need to understand the value of that as well. It's not just sticking up photos and leave them to it is there. There's a philosophy behind that as well.

Debi Keyte-Hartland: There is. That's right. And I think you know what they were interested in - because of course, they were then videoing what the children were doing, which is another part of the pedagogical process. They filmed it in order to try and understand how children made friends with each other at such a young age.

What were the connections that they made to the images?

Did they notice them?

Could they find themselves?

Could they find a friend within those images?

So that's why I call it a research methodology in that you're actually trying to find something out about children so that then you can offer that back to them.

Kathy Brodie: Yes and that's the important other half of the circle. Capturing that it's them - then what do you do with that. As you said at the beginning, offering it back to the children. How would you offer it back to very young babies how would you then share that back again?

Debi Keyte-Hartland: Well I've certainly done things where I put things on the floor so especially with images or with film. Often it's to offer it back in a slightly different context, so that they can see themselves.

I saw some wonderful work in a Swedish pre-school. With their youngest children, they'd noticed how they were banging pots and pans outside in the garden, as children do, with various spoons and whisks and they filmed this. Then they brought the film back inside and they projected it really large in this space and in front of the projection of the film was the pots and pans and (not drumsticks and things, I would've put drumsticks in) but they were so close to the children's ideas that they put the spoons and the whisks back in. They then re-invited the children back into that context so that the children could see themselves in the garden. But it also got the materials that they could interact with themselves. So it was a beautiful thing.

Kathy Brodie: How fantastic what a great idea. Reacting immediately is so important as well. Not, we'll do that next week on the planning, it has got to be almost instant hasn't it to pick up on the children's ideas?

Debi Keyte-Hartland: In that moment of self reflection, when sometimes you're thinking about it at the time, of working with the kids children, want you could be doing next or what you could offer next. Sometimes you need to take it to your group or to your colleagues and talk it through, in order to try and figure out what to do next.

It was like Malaguzzi of the schools in Reggio Emilia always said – 'to stand aside for a while and listen carefully and perhaps teaching would be different than before'. And for me that's what pedagogical documentation is about. It is about standing aside just for a while, but not being the adult who can't be interacted with, just to notice what children are doing and then make decisions based on that rather than just pulling ideas out of the air.

I think if we are pulling ideas out of the air, we're not thinking about the child in front of us and therefore we might be at danger of a disconnect. And for me that doesn't help them with that personal social and emotional well-being.

Kathy Brodie: Absolutely. I think that the days are long gone, thank goodness, where we did planning in the summer holidays for next year even before we met the children. It's that immediacy and that standing back.

Even just having a notebook next to you and writing it down, having to think to put that into a form of words and physically write it down. That does give you that second or two of reflection to think "where this is going? what's important? why am I noting this in particular about this group of children or this particular child?"

That's what pedagogical documentation is and some really nice examples there. What strategies can practitioners and educators out there right now start to use in order to implement it? I know it's not as easy as just 'tomorrow we're going to be doing pedagogical documentation' but what are some of the simple strategies they can start to employ to bring that into their settings?

Debi Keyte-Hartland: Well, I think it's important to realize that they're probably already doing some of it. They will already be taking photographs or maybe some films.

What I always say is to start small and Gunilla Dahlberg, she often talks about 'taking tiny ant steps' so as not to overwhelm yourself. So I would suggest to take an ant's step and maybe to have in mind a possible research question, which could be 'How do children form relationships through their play'. Something as simple as that. Or 'what are the strategies are the children using to get to know one another'.

Then I'd have a nice note book - go out and buy a nice notebook or a file or whatever it is that does it for you. And I'd have something that was nothing too big, nothing that was going to cause a barrier between you and the children. (I think clipboards are like a miniature wall that we put up between children). I'd have it by my side. And I would sit with a group of children and just listen and begin to be part of listening to their conversation and just take note of their actions in relation to your question or your theory that you might have about children.

Then I'd find somebody and talk about what's I've seen because it's in that coming together with somebody else where you find out that there's a different perspective. They might have seen that child in a different situation that connects. It might help you see patterns of behaviour that's happening across different places.

And then I would simply share back the photographs with the children themselves. And often I would do that from a book. So, "this was you last time. Have you seen what you're doing here here?" It opens up a conversation.

Alternatively, you might want to take short films. You can gather a lot of information from films. Children love seeing the films back, and for the families of course. I only take it for five minutes at a time. If you take a 30 minute film you've got to spend 30 minutes, a good half an hour, actually watching it back. I take short snippets of film, either one minute pieces of film and allow yourself five snippets or five minutes of continuous film.

Then afterwards watch it and see what that brings up for you in terms of what those children are doing. I think in that way, as long as we are reflecting on the material that we are collecting, then we are automatically thinking about what we can do next for children. That will mean that we're by their side instead of leading out from the front.

Kathy Brodie: Yes, I think that that's obviously the key. It is that process, a joint process. As you say you're by the by your side. I love the idea of reflecting with your colleagues on that.

I can imagine as a staff group that would be really nice, or a childminding network, to take that along to a network meeting. Somebody else look at it and say "Did you notice that they were doing that again?" "I didn't even see that".

Certainly when I've been doing research and we've reviewed video, it's the things that other people notice that make you think "oh yeah". And that's what kind of changes your perspective does it.

Debi Keyte-Hartland: And it becomes part of our professional development then. It's continuing professional development, if we're doing that on an everyday basis.

I think one of the important things is in showing back with the children is that they get to see their ideas side by side by other children. And it helps them see that there are multiple perspectives, that there are different points of view. In a way we are modelling that democratic process, that we don't always have to think about the same, it's not about all about being the same. We can accept our differences and our similarities and look for connections and patterns between us.

Kathy Brodie: Of course, that's the core of a lot of what we do.

You can call it unique child or British Values or whatever. But that's the real bedrock. This is how we are as a community. And that's obviously going to vary from setting to setting, situation to situation. And I'm guessing from cohort of children to children. I guess that children are going to react to those things differently as well?

Debi Keyte-Hartland: Absolutely yes.

Kathy Brodie: I just think that's a really nice idea. And in a minute of video you can get an awful lot in. I'm thinking if they're playing outside, - doing a lot of things actually – in a minute video you can see lots and lots going on. I just think that would be a really nice thing. And just to review some of those together with the children.

Debi Keyte-Hartland: It's on a bigger scale as well. It's like going into the cinema and seeing yourself in action there where.

Kathy Brodie: You could just hang a sheet on the wall. I think that's a really nice idea and very visual. So that's a good way to learn and have that joint learning process. There are some really nice ideas.

What would your top tip be for practitioners who wanted to look into pedagogical documentation and find out more about it? Where would they go and what would your top tip be for looking into?

Debi Keyte-Hartland: Well, I would always start in going back to one of the main sources of pedagogical documentation and look at some of the early examples from Reggio Emilia. I also write and blog a lot about pedagogical documentation so you could look there too.

Kathy Brodie: On your website www.debikeytehartland.me And you can find out more information there.

Debi Keyte-Hartland: But the important thing is to not just read lots and lots and lots about it, but just to go and start doing it. We're already doing part of that process, through our formative and observational assessments already. It's just taking that next leap to seeing how can we use it directly with the children and how can I use it to better understand children and to plan what to do next.

Kathy Brodie: Yes and I think that's something I meant to mention, that planning can often be seen as "oh it's Thursday afternoon we've got to do the planning" and obviously that's going to be going out the window isn't it. Because you'll be planning the whole time that'll be a very dynamic process won't it.

Debi Keyte-Hartland: Oh that's right.

Kathy Brodie: How would you actually put that on planning, how would you present that as a piece of planning?

Debi Keyte-Hartland: In using books, for example following up from the last time you were with children. You will have an idea of what to do next. So I would simply just write it on the next page. Today we're looking at you know blah blah… in relation to what we did last time.

I wouldn't necessarily have all the paperwork, but what you end up with is a chronological book that tracks developments and then uses the planning cycle of the reflective cycle all in all in. You know, nobody says that planning has to be done on a Thursday afternoon there.

Kathy Brodie: I know!! That's just what happens…

Debi Keyte-Hartland: Yeah, neither does it say that we have to plan for all individual children, but we can look at what's interesting those in those individuals, as we look at connections and other things that are of interest to children.

Kathy Brodie: I think that that's really the heart of it - following that child's lead. Following those interests. I'm really cueing into what it is that they're interested in, having it as a process and working alongside the children you're naturally going to be meeting their interests.

I really like the idea of having a research question in your book as well because that means that there is some *aim* rather than "oh let's get the play dough I've not had the play dough out for a while" but this is *why* we're getting it out.

Debi Keyte-Hartland: And what is it that you want to find out?

I met a teacher in my first visit to Reggio Emilia and she'd been working for 20 years as a school with children aged three to six. She just moved into working with children aged one to three. She said "I've got 20 years of experience of working with children. But each day I try to find out something that I didn't know before".

Kathy Brodie: That's pretty powerful isn't it.

Debi Keyte-Hartland: So you are seeing yourself as a researcher, trying to find out how children develop, how they form relationships with one another, how they become interested in things and how they express what they know about the world.

Kathy Brodie: I just think that's an absolutely fascinating topic and it makes so much sense. I'm really pleased it's not quite as scary as I thought it might be when we said we were looking at pedagogical documentation. I certainly love the idea of videoing children and having a nice book.

You've already mentioned that you do have a website www.debikeytehartland.me and there's tons of information on there, for your publications and things that are coming up as well, that's all on there.

187

I really like on your site is a Tedx Brum talk, which is based in Birmingham in the U.K., and that's a really nice little video. About 15 minutes talking about visual creativity.

It has been absolutely fascinating. Thank you so, so much for joining us today. I am really going to go and have a look at more pedagogical documentation and find out more about that. But thank you for the moment. Thank you very much indeed, Debi Keyte-Hartland for joining us on the Early Years Web Summit.

Debi Keyte-Hartland: Thank you. Thank you very much.

CHAPTER 11

CHILDREN'S MENTAL HEALTH

Wendy Baker

Kathy Brodie: I'm really excited to be joined by Wendy Baker. Wendy has worked in the earlier sector for 25 years as a nursery practitioner, nursery manager and area manager, working both private and state sectors in nurseries and schools.

She has three back to back 'Outstanding' Ofsted inspections - I can't think of anyone else who has got that, so that's pretty amazing. Wendy has done troubleshooting and crisis management and works now as a freelance Early Years consultant, offering a number of different training courses and consultancy services. Her courses are around children's well-being and mental health and she's really interested in anxiety. She runs a number of popular Facebook groups that are close to her heart.

Welcome to the Early Years Web Summit Wendy Baker.

Wendy Baker: Thank you very much Kathy.

Kathy Brodie: You're very welcome. Today we're going to be focussing on personal, social and emotional development. But the thing I really want to look at most is children's own identity and children's mental health and how that all fits into the personal, social and emotional development area. So let's start with children's identities, Wendy can you tell me a little more about what this means please?

Wendy Baker: I think it really means Kathy, that it is how children see themselves and how other children see them. So thinking about how they are within themselves. How they value themselves, their self esteem and their self-awareness and obviously the child being that unique child. What makes that child them?

That's also culture but also in their family as well, so not just that the oldest child or the youngest child, but how they are perceived within their family and also obviously within the settings as well. It's really important that we know that as key people.

It's also about how they talk about themselves and what they're proud of and how they're proud of their achievements. It's how they're building relationships and being part of a bigger community. How they behave within that. About learning about boundaries and rules within society and how they will behave within society as well. So I think it's really around that Kathy.

If I may talk about the adult's role in that because obviously that's important. It's about valuing and respecting the child's which is absolutely paramount. And then also us being positive role models, to set good examples to children so that children know that they feel valued and listened to, that people are going to actually listen to what they're saying. A child might pick up the courage to go "I'm going to say something to Wendy" and then Wendy might be, unfortunately, a little bit busy. There's a missed opportunity and that child might not feel reassured and not have the confidence to go and speak to you next time, because she hasn't listened to us.

I think that's quite important in settings, especially when we're quite busy, as much as we try. It's really important we try and do that with children.

Giving adults the opportunity to work with children about how they see themselves so, in small groups talking about feelings, emotions, about their identity and how they see themselves as well. And we need to make sure that we're also being positive role models in our behaviour towards the children and also other adults and colleagues ourselves.

So it's about praise and support, guiding and encouraging them but also celebrating their achievements as well. And I'll just finish with, we know that the Early Years framework in the U.K.

says that unique child, it talks about each child being unique and they should be resilient, capable, confident and self-assured.

Kathy Brodie: Those few words cover an awful lot don't they? But as you say there's a massive role that as the practitioners can play in supporting that. So if we are thinking about mental health and children's mental health in our settings, how can we monitor children's mental health? what sort of things are we looking for when we're looking at that?

Wendy Baker: Well first of all Kathy, children display all types of different behaviour, so it doesn't just mean that a child is going to necessarily have a mental illness or mental health problems. In Early Years children have all types of different behaviours, for different reasons. Like adults, children experience anxiety at different times in their lives, which is normal, but it's about how we, as adults, support those children with those transitions.

For example, the child's going off to school. Are we supporting them with books, talking about their school visits to the school and then working in partnership with parents as well to support that. And it's about how we're dealing with that as adults. How those children's experiences will be, whether it be positive or negative, will also impact on their further life outcomes and how they deal with their own emotions.

It's important to remember that mental health problems, unfortunately, are on the increase or maybe we've also a greater awareness, which is good. Two mental health charities are 'Young Minds' which do a hell of a lot of work with children and young people. And their mission is really about children's emotional well-being and mental health. And many years ago I actually read my first article from Young Minds and it talked about children as young as two actually being depressed. So that's really quite significant back then and I think from then I've always had a bigger understanding and interest in children's well-being and mental health. 'A Place to Be' is another amazing charity that supports children in both primary and secondary schools through counselling in one on one to ones and also in small groups and also working with the families.

If we look at the statistics - just two statistics that I'm going to share with you - it's quite alarming actually. So one in 10 children between the ages of five to 16, that's three children in every class room, has a mental health problem. That's really, really high. This is from the data of the 'Children's to be' statistics. This may continue into adulthood, it doesn't mean they're all going to continue that.

Another startling statistic is the *significant* mental health before issues before the age of 14.

We're at the forefront of early intervention in Early Years so it's really important that we are very aware of children's well-being and mental health, so we can support them, so that they get their opportunities and services and can access those. So that doesn't impact on their further learning and also their emotional well-being and their outcomes as adults. And that's really important.

Those statistics are quite high, but with those charities and now, and we know that the Duke and Duchess of Cambridge and Prince Harry are looking at mental health, which is good because that will highlight and support mental health and give it a better name so we can help children and people.

How do we monitor it? We monitor that through safeguarding, which is paramount in the setting, the wellbeing of each child and very much the effective key worker system. It's not just about keeping the records and settling in the children, it's about do we really know our role and responsibilities? And I do sometimes see in settings that sometimes key people who don't, for some reason, like that they've got too many key children, there's a lot of pressure. And I understand that. But it's about really, really knowing our role and a big part of our role is about consistency and making sure that we build secure attachments with those children.

Some children don't have any consistency in their in their home lives. They might start off coming to nursery or child minders in the morning by the time they have gone home, they might actually have moved house but there are other reasons. It happens and lots of children are living in really difficult, often difficult, complex backgrounds. Ensuring that the nursery or the child minder setting might be the only consistency that they actually see. So our role as a key person is absolutely vital about making sure we know each child individually and it's not just about what they like and their preferences. The real little things that upsets them, how are they going to react things, how they deal with change. It's about that rapport and been in tune with children which absolutely is key.

It's also about supporting your key children if they are going through a difficult time, through changes. It's also working in partnership with parents, making sure that you have real one to one with parents so that you know what's going on. And how you can support both the family, but also the child through those difficulties as well.

I would also say really good observations and documentation and sometimes it's also not just written observations, it can be about your children, for example when they might not be feeling well because they might be off their food. I'm looking for those little significant changes and things in which what they're saying to you and their behaviour and how they're behaving within the setting.

And as we know through observations it's about those cohort

sheets. Are they making significant progress and if a child isn't, what we need to do. We know that Ofsted are looking for that and making sure that how are we supporting those most vulnerable children to achieve progress and making sure that we are supporting them to get the early intervention. So that's really important as well.

Kathy Brodie: I think that's a really interesting point that you make about the families. We don't always know what's going on. And certainly I've had conversations with people about homelessness. We tend to think about that as living on the streets but in fact there might be families out there who are moving from friends to friends to friends because they don't have a home of their own for a multitude of reasons. But unless you start to make those connections you're never going to find that out and that's going to have a significant effect on a child. As you say, if they don't even know where they're going back to when they're going to what they call home. I can't imagine what that would do to a child's mental health.

So that's really interesting you have to make those real life connections it's not just the paperwork, you've got to dig a little bit deeper. So in practical terms and what sort of top tips could you give for practitioners and educators to support children so that they do have that very good mental health and support in their personal, social and emotional development?

Wendy Baker: It starts with a really good knowledge and understanding of child development and what that really means. And so staff keep up to date with that and also attachment. What does it mean to have secure attachments with children?

We need to keep looking at that as practitioners and reflecting on that. An understanding of what is mental health and well-being, so making sure SENCOs and staff are going on training. And I know that there's a lot of training out there for schools and there's just been, in the UK, some more money that could be going into schools. That's brilliant, but we also need it to filter down to Early Years as well which is vital.

Also training in Child Trauma. And I'd like to actually mention an amazing expert in this, and I know she's on the Early Years Summit as well this year, Jane Evans. I've seen her talking, she's an absolutely amazing expert in child trauma and also in anxiety. And she really talks that in Early Years we need to be having training in trauma. When I trained many years ago, trauma wasn't really spoken about. We might have a little bit about children's 'difficult circumstances'. But that was really it. We didn't have a lot. So it's about also accessing them and there's lots of amazing websites out there. And please look up Jane because she is amazing.

Then the charities that I spoke about they do significant work and they also have access to training courses. But it's about you, your work with children, and it's about how you perceive children.

It's about going back to that effective key worker system, really being in tune with your children. Working in partnership with parents as well with the children and also respecting them as well as making sure that you know children are making significant progress.

It's about effective leadership so that managers and leaders are monitoring children, and some staff's progress, with their children's profiles and making sure that if children are having some significant lack in progress then what you're actually doing about that. And you can talk about that in supervisions as well.

From a practical side you can do things like add a well-being boards in your setting that supports parents about helping to raise awareness of children's well-being with things that they can do at home with their child. Staff have got boards, maybe in a staff room, and access to information that they can look at things. Obviously the staff's well-being is absolutely vital in this as well. And we need to be in a good place ourselves.

I'm a great believer in transition songs. Children need to make sure that they know what's happening next. We sometimes, with best will in the world, forget with children and think that "It's okay. They'll just go along with it". But we need to tell children what's happening next. What's going on. Their settings are their second homes and its important that they really know what's going on, so visual boards and timetables. I'm really a great believer in those things.

I am going back to the transitional songs, about cleaning your teeth etc. just helping and it also supports children with EAL as well.

Looking at your environment, definitely. My last setting was upstairs and downstairs so children did a lot of transitions and that can have a big impact on their well-being and also their play and learning, if they keep having to go up and down stairs. It's bad enough for us, but for that little child it's worse. Really look at our environment and how we could change that.

Making sure it's a calm environment as possible as it can be. Nurseries are busy, but making sure that children have got security and consistency with that.

The way in which we approach settling in of children and information that we're gathering, that builds that rapport with not just the child but the parents. So some things that we used to do was 'All About Me Box'. It was a little cardboard box and staff would just have significant things in there. For example my box was very much about where I lived. I came to nursery on a train and I lived in a flat and I had a cat. So you're sharing this with the key child and the parents. And what happens is you're building that rapport up, you're developing that relationship. So parents hopefully will open up to you about things as well.

We used to put a little picture of the key person on the jam jar lids and the key child could take that home with them. So they then felt supported that they could then say "I am going to go and see Kathy tomorrow" and "Kathy is going to be looking after me" and the parent can then talk to the child so the transition – it's a big thing going to nursery or child minders away from your family - then they can support them in that way.

It's about as key people really, really knowing our key children, being in tune and I can't really stress that enough. I mean we do that a lot, but sometimes we need to remember those really significant things about children and how their behaviour is going to affect certain things and sometimes how we are in tune with their behaviour as well.

Kathy Brodie: I think that's a really really nice idea to practitioners to have their own box. I mean I've done it the other way where children bring in significant things. But of course we should be doing that, we should be sharing. I know that I've worked in places and maybe the parents aren't too sure of your name, maybe a name badge wasn't on when you first arrived. And then after about week three they're a bit embarrassed to say "oh what's your name". And so it goes on. So making that exchange and just having pictures in the hallway all those sorts of things for parents make it so much easier to have those real genuine connections. I think those boxes are a great idea. I wish I'd know that before. Have you got any examples of that sort of working please?

Wendy Baker: At my last setting we worked with a child who came to us when he was two and basically the family had quite significant issues. And as we got to know that family it became more apparent that dad actually had mental health issues. Some professionals have been involved, but it was quite a difficult situation. We could see - the key person, the SENCO and obviously myself - that there was real significant delay in his three Prime Areas, particularly communication and language and also his personal, social and emotional development.

He was very withdrawn in the setting. He didn't like anybody to approach them. He didn't actually know how to do certain things. He didn't have any spoken words at all, even though his attention and listening was absolutely fine. So we had to work with him and how we did that was to work with the parents.

With the parent's permission, we worked with our local authority and we also did what was formerly known as the Common Assessment Framework and we worked with other professionals from health and also the SENCO team to support his needs and the family needs and that went on for two years. But within that two years that child did make progress and that's fantastic. But very much his mental stability. He didn't have a relationship with his mum, which was really very sad, she'd have post-natal depression and had not been diagnosed.

So we had to really support the family and it's about attachment. Sometimes it's that whole bigger picture and we know in Early Years that we have to do that but it's making sure that we're aware of that within Early Years. We know that we're doing fantastic work, but we know that we need to do more to make a real difference to each child.

Kathy Brodie: If we do observations and we do identify that maybe there is something that's troubling something's not quite right here. What would your advice be on the first steps? How would you then progressed from that kind of little niggly feeling?

Wendy Baker: Well obviously you would get your SENCO to come down and also do your observations as well. And then share what the setting SENCO said with the key person. Then speak to the parents - always seek a parental permission obviously. Then you could have a meeting with the parents and either the parents could access their GP or their health visitor.

The two year old check is really significant here, as we know, and then go to your local authority. We went to our SENCO team and they were able to help us. But we know there's lots of cuts going on now and it could be quite difficult. So it's really important that we make those strong links and obviously with health as well.

With the two year old check and hopefully the integrated check in the UK we're going to be seeing a lot more significance with that. I know the 2 year old check is really significant and most certainly helped us identify, along with our observations, other the children's needs. And also you know the cohort sheets where children were not making progress.

Kathy Brodie: So that was already having an effect, because in the UK the two year old checks only really been around for a few years but that's really interesting. I think that's across the world really that at about age 2 if things aren't developing or progressing or if there's a plateau then you can start to see that that you're kind of either caught up or something's going on at age 2.

That's interesting that the two year old progress check as a formal check in the U.K. is actually having an effect.

Tell me a little bit about the courses that you do Wendy.

Wendy Baker: Well I do a course around children's mental health and well-being. So we very much look at the children's rights going back to the UN Rights of the Child Act, which the UK does and we very much cover about what is children's wellbeing, look at attachment and also look at our role as a key person. Also identifying lots about anxiety and how we can support children so very much similar things in more detail of what we've talked about today.

Then also I do another training course around babies and under twos. And we're very much looking at attachment theory there and our role and a positive interactions. So I do training around those.

Kathy Brodie: It's really good to hear that you actually do specific mental health courses. I know that in a lot of courses, it's mentioned somewhere down the road but to actually have a whole course about children's mental health, I think is absolutely excellent. And as you say, unfortunately needed more and more or maybe we're just identifying it better, I'm on the fence on that at the moment. it's really good to see that there is somewhere where you can go to get a course and actually learn all about that. It has been fascinating talking with you Wendy. Thank you so so much for joining us today. I'm going to go away and think about what I am going to put in my practitioners box. Thank you Wendy for joining us on the Early Years web summit.

Wendy Baker: Thank you very much.

CHAPTER 12

THE REGGIO EMILIA APPROACH AND PSED

Suzanne Axelsson

Kathy Brodie: I'm really excited to be joined by Suzanne Axelsson. Suzanne has more than 20 years experience in a variety of Early Years settings multilingual Reggio Emilia, traditional Swedish settings as well as Montessori settings. On her blog 'Interaction, Imagination' she shares ideas experiences and ponderings, all about working in the Early Years. Until recently Suzanne worked in Sweden's first pre-school with a philosophical profile, where she developed how philosophy can act as a pedagogical tool for young children. Most recently Suzanne has been involved in the freedom theatre in Jenin, Palestine. In an effort to inspire a greater play focus on early childhood education in Jenin, as an adviser from Sweden, as well as on site support teacher training and researching the effectiveness of this course I I'm delighted to have you here. Welcome to the summit Suzanne.

Suzanne Axelsson: Thank you for having me.

Kathy Brodie: a great pleasure. I'm absolutely thrilled that you're able to join us because I want to explore the Reggio Emilia approach with you today and particularly how that can support young children's personal, social and emotional development.

Suzanne Axelsson: I think the whole idea of the Reggio Emilia approach is a very social one. It's about relationships. It's about the pedagogy of listening. So by enabling children to be able to listen not only to the teacher, but to each other, and their teachers being able to listen better to the children. You establish the social emotional relationships within the whole group with each individual child, and the teacher relationship with each child. There is a focus on group learning.

I like the word 'we' because it's not just the idea each individual child the 'me' of each child, but it's also the 'we' it's learning together and that learning is not a separate thing. I know in England there's this wonderful word 'unique' child. And I struggle with that a little bit because I know each child has their own individual way of learning but 'unique' seems to separate them all off into their own little categories. While I want the learning should be a community rather than individual and that our differences gives us new perspectives that we can learn from each other. We do that together, rather than in our unique ways. So we take this uniqueness, our differences, as a strength that we can share with each other. And then it becomes like a natural part of society, a natural part of learning instead of all these different ways of learning. Even though there is the hundred languages of Reggio Emilia it's not saying that we have to treat each of these hundred languages separately, it's using all of these languages together and seeing them as a strength.

Kathy Brodie: Stronger together rather than as separate then..

Suzanne Axelsson: Yes, very much so. It's typical Vygotsky, each child will learn from each other, they will support each other. Then the adult should be scaffolding their learning rather than we are informing the children how to learn and filling them with information. The children are co-constructing their own knowledge and very much active in this whole learning process, which means because they're doing this together, their social emotional skills are developing at the same time as they're constructing knowledge.

Kathy Brodie: There is very much a focus on that social aspect of the personal social emotional development isn't there.

So whenever I see a Reggio Emilia setting, when I see pictures and videos of the environment that's going on, it always seems quite busy and quite purposeful. But first could you give us just a brief overview of what the Reggio Emilia approach is and how that translates into Early Years practice. What you would expect to see in a setting following this philosophy?

Suzanne Axelsson: It started at the end of the Second World War when the women of Reggio Emilia did not want their children to just follow a dictator blindly again. They wanted their children to think critically, that there should be democracy. They asked Malaguzzi, who was only 24 years old at the time, to support them in teaching their children a way to become democratic members of society and critical thinkers. He obviously was very humble in this, saying - well, I don't know how to do this but, I can learn together as the children learn. Children will teach me. And I think use this is as a 'teaching back' tool.

It started there and he basically looked at all the different kinds of research from Dewey, Piaget, Froebel - you name it he's looked at it. Hawkins is one of my favourites too. And he took pieces of all of these different kinds of pedagogies and methods and pieced them together. It suited the children and the setting and the context they were in and not just within pedagogical study - he went into psychology and sociology. If he were still here now, I'm quite sure Alison Gopnick and brain research would infiltrate his research and be woven into this fabric.

He was very, very clear that this was not a method. It was an approach, that we shouldn't be writing this down because this pedagogy should be evolving all the time, in the same way that society evolves, in the same way that children evolve. So we can't fix it and say this is a 'right' and 'wrong 'way of doing it. We should always be piecing things together to create the right learning circumstances for the group of children in the context you're working in right now.

Kathy Brodie: Is that the physical environment as well as how educators and practitioners work with the children?

Suzanne Axelsson: Absolutely. There's the social environment, the physical environment, the cultural environment.

The children are not just part of the school - they have their family, their home, they have their neighbourhood, they have their city they have their own region, their country and also part of the world. All of this influences them. The child is not just what they are in school but he has to take part of everything in the context what happens in Italy is not the same as what's happening to me here in Stockholm, which is definitely not the same as what's happening back in the UK.

We all have to have our different approaches and both in Italy and Sweden, we don't start school until much later than what you do in the UK. So we have more time to do as use these kind of approaches of not forcing reading and writing. Which is wonderful - we do it when the children are interested and that really means that we can focus more energy on the social emotional welfare of the children because we're doing things when they are ready for it, rather than when they HAVE to do it because policy in the school says 'now you have to learn to read' and regardless of whether the child is ready.

Kathy Brodie: You're laying down those foundations aren't you that bedrock. And then when they do get to school or get to formal education then they can fly can't they because that's always sort of lay laid down for them.

So, that's a bit of a flavour of where it came from, the sorts of things you would expect to see in that approach. How does that vary with other pedagogy because you've heard you mentioned quite a few other people there, which I'm sure a lot of our listeners and viewers will be familiar with. So what do you think the main differences are between the pedagogies are?

Suzanne Axelsson: I think a lot of the pedagogies are methods rather than approaches. Therefore is quite this thing of being a 'right or wrong' approach. This is a 'Montessori way' of doing it so it needs to be done this, take out the mats and they should not be used as stepping stones because they are a work surface. You carry the chair like this... I think there's a lot of good points in Montessori. I love the way that ergonomics is a very important way, that carrying this chair is not just about doing it correctly, it's about supporting their backs and so it is much more complex.

I personally struggle with the Montessori method. It has a 'correct way' of using blocks in a 'correct way' of using the mats because in my head I was wanting to use them as stepping stones, especially when they are all dotted around. Or when they were not being used as work surfaces but at other times to be used, but they couldn't because they were 'holy' in that sense. And of course I think if Maria Montessori was alive now she would do it very differently. Meeting the needs of children now. These are the needs of children a hundred years ago and I think she was revolutionary at the time. She is amazing and there's so much that is still incredibly relevant to today. But I think we need to build on it and I think Reggio gives you that edge to be able to just take the parts that are relevant to yourself, rather than having to follow the entire method, if you agree with it or not.

Kathy Brodie: In that respect it is actually a true pedagogy isn't it, because it is an approach, rather than having to sort of tick those boxes or meet those needs for something that you might be following. And I'm particularly thinking here of the English curriculum under the EYFS, that we feel we've got to follow that quite rigid framework in some ways but in fact Reggio allows you, well it encourages you, to actually go outside that box and to think about different things that the children might want to explore and particularly in their environment as well. Could you give us a little bit of a flavour of what a Reggio Emilia environment would look like, what you would expect to see in there?

Suzanne Axelsson: And is this something I can joke around a lot with, really because I think there's a big focus on Reggio Emilia's environments being beautiful and everything has been beautiful and wooden and natural and I do not think this is the case. I think it should be put together with care with respect for the children. What is beautiful? Is it from an adult perspective? Is it from a child's perspective? So I question that. That's when I look at what they have constructed with blocks as beautiful – it is sometimes, but I have to have a leap of imagination there to find beauty.

I think it's being a space that is designed to create interactions between the children and the adults. So that they can learn together is a space that creates opportunities for the children to come together and learn together as well but also opportunities to go off and explore on their own. Its a space to allow them to be competent. They can make choices. So everything has to be considered carefully.

How are you putting things on the shelves?

Why are these things close together, why not these things close together? So just choices.

Always as a teacher you're reflecting on why am I making the room like this?

Why am I dividing it into construction area and a writing corner?

Why is the writing corner over in this side of the room?

The construction over on this side of the room?

And how do these interact with each other?

Could I change the dynamics by putting them closer together. or mixing them together?

Kathy Brodie: So just by actually setting up your environment and thinking about where things are, you're actually changing maybe, the way that children access things, the way that they make those connections and they might even come up with some surprising connections which we've never thought of before. Simply by moving the writing next to the construction area or something like that.

Suzanne Axelsson: We found that the construction and the role play area needs to be really close together because they wanted to mix those materials together all the time. And we have experimented like crazy, sometimes we had the opposite ends of the building and the children were just transport everything from the construction area into the role play area or vice versa - little handbags were perfect for putting in blocks in and things like that and all of these materials. And they could be transported. I mean transportation is just brilliant as it is, but it often made it hard to find where everything was at the end of the day and sorting became tricky.

So we're trying to enable the children to have a space that was easy for them to manage as well. A lot of people discuss this whole idea of a 'messy' environment. And I think mess can sometimes be a sign of play. It's not a bad thing but when you're drawing you prefer to draw on a blank piece of paper to get your own creativity not always to be recycling old drawings on newspapers as you are drawing paper and then I think it's the same with play. It's fine to move into a room that shows a lot of evidence of play and it's chaotic. You can carry on the play but there is also that need for the room be set up in a way that you can start a new play if you want to. This needs to be a combination of both.

Kathy Brodie: Again, it's that thought that practitioners and educators need to put into it to stand back and have a look at the environment and just say what am I trying to achieve? It might be you've got to leave out the models that they've made because you want them to carry on or the children would like them left. Or it might be that you make that decision that, no today we're going to start with a blank canvas and start again here.

Suzanne Axelsson: Usually you can tell when you need a blank canvas because no one's going to that table any more.

Kathy Brodie: I see, that's interesting. Right. So that moves us quite nicely on top tips for practitioners what sort of thing should they'd be looking for. Because at the moment it's sounding quite complicated. You've got to do a lot of reflection a lot of thinking about, but that's a really great top tip already, that if they're not going back to that table to play with it they're actually telling you - I've had enough of that you need to do something else out there.

Suzanne Axelsson: Yeah. I tidy it up and put it away and have another invitation available or just a blank space so that they can start again and bring out their own ideas. Putting up photographs of what there was there up on the wall next to it or creating a file next to it so they can see. We did this with Lego, because Lego is one of those materials that often is hard pressed and there is sometimes quite a lot of competition with who gets the best pieces. Lego is really really good but, when we do have Lego we will take photographs of the children's creations and we made a book of it and the children could go back and look at it. So there wasn't this need to save it forever so that they could save it through these books. And then we often would look through these books and use them as inspirations. The children would be inspired by someone else's creation.

If there was time you'd just load a photograph into a PowerPoint get the child to describe what it was. So you just have a brief amount of text then you just print out. I mean especially when you have access to the wifi printing system where you could be there with your laptop with the child. Print it out go collect it and stick it in their file.

Kathy Brodie: It's instant then isn't it. That's a really super idea. I love the idea of taking photos. That doesn't have to just be Lego. You can expand that to anything couldn't you. Outdoor play in all sorts of different things there.

Suzanne Axelsson: We do this with excursions and with activities and with all sorts of things about 'what do you remember from yesterday', we can put it into their portfolio as well so it makes it simpler and the children become aware of why we're documenting. So then they also become more aware of telling you "you need to take a photograph of this because I'm learning how to do this". My children became experts "you need to film this", and they knew the difference between when I had to film them and when I had to take a photograph of them as well because they knew which was the process and which was a memory.

They become experts in documenting themselves. Because I shared the documentation process WITH the children rather than doing it separately.

Kathy Brodie: So that must have taken time though, you must have taken time to sit with the child and explain what you're doing and taking them through that.

Suzanne Axelsson: All the time: "I'm taking this photograph so that you can see later". And sometimes they would draw pictures and they'd say "you need to take a photograph of this picture because in six months time I want to do the same kind of picture, I want to see how I have grown in my learning" because they'd seen that I'm done this. Because I worked with the same children for three years, they also learned my learning style and teaching style. So they were able to use and exploit me to the best extent, as well, which is what Reggio Emilia is about. This is a relationship between a teacher and the child to optimize learning.

Kathy Brodie: I think that's another benefit for having children for that bit longer before they start formal schooling because you've got that bit of extra time to build those relationships up as well.

Suzanne Axelsson: Even in the Swedish school system, a class teacher will have their children for three years.

Kathy Brodie: Oh how super. So as you say they will they will get to know you in that time won't they. Is that quite a standard thing?

Suzanne Axelsson: Yes, that's standard. When they get older then they'll have different teachers for different subjects but they will have the same mentor teacher for three years.

Kathy Brodie: I think that's a really, really good idea because by the time you're in the first year, if you're just with a teacher for one year, you've only really just got to know them and then you have to go through the transitions again.

So if you've got practitioners and viewers who are watching at the moment and they're thinking this sounds this would fit me really well. How would you advise somebody to start a Reggio Emilia approach in their setting - or is it that easy?

Suzanne Axelsson: I think yes and no. If you make the decision that its something you want to do, then, yes it's easy you throw yourself into it.

But no, it's not easy because it's not so instant. It's a *process* and it takes many, many years and I am still in my process. I am still learning and I've been doing this... I'm not even going to say how many years!

You've got to dare to make mistakes. You've got to dare to let go of the power and it's not about following the child. It's about having an equal power with the child. You are empowering the child for their own learning. I am not teaching the child, we are learning together - I am enabling their learning. This a very different approach in that sense. I see a lot of teachers that are kind of nervous of giving up that power because as adults we have an enormous amount of power and being aware of how much power you have in the room really helps that balance to become more equal.

I had children that one year, seriously challenged my authority. They were just saying why are you making all the decisions? why can't we make all the decisions? Children being children, they don't realise making decisions means you also have to take responsibility for these decisions. And when I make decisions I take responsibility for that. So I handed over the power to them and said, "You're making the decisions" and they did not like the responsibility that came with it. They found it too hard work and they would much rather play than take responsibility of choosing, of going to make sure that everyone was included.

There was one time where it just went crazy and a couple of children started hitting each other and I was thinking, "Oh my God what if I done?" It was the scariest 10 minutes of my life because I was thinking – "I have gone mad. I should not have done this, what are the parents go to say?" within this 10 minutes the children came to me. "You've got to take control again. You've got to tell him to stop now." Well no you said you wanted the control. This means that you need to tell him to stop. And he came up "They're not listening to me, they're not listening to me". So we had this huge dialogue afterwards about what I had, what my control was, I was ensuring that they were safe, that they were all able to have their voices heard by everyone, that each child was respected and valued. I wasn't making them do anything. I was just empowering the children themselves wanted.

Kathy Brodie: That's a very significant difference. I think that's something that educators still struggle with. Am I following the children's leads? Am I actually putting my own adult agenda on what it is that we're doing here?

I think that's happening every day in settings up and down the country where educators are saying "Am I going to step in or am I going to stand back they're going to have to sort this out?"

That's really interesting that you then had the dialogue afterwards with the children and explained that. And that's for me maybe is the Reggio Emilia approach there.

Suzanne Axelsson: It is the dialogues and this is why working philosophically was so empowering as well because as you're not a leader of a dialogue, you were a facilitator of the children's dialogue. So during the actual philosophical dialogue itself my opinions were not to be put across at all. I am not to have a hidden agenda. I am just there to listen and to enable their thinking to help the children connect their thinking.

They were two years old when they started - the youngest child was two years old - and so they did this until half the group was six and they started school and I documented, I wrote down every single dialogue we had with the children and you can not only see their language developments you can see their idea developments you can see their social development.

Now all of this is visible in these texts, but you also had to enforce a strict routine of rule within the dialogue that you keep on topic. You always respect all of each other's ideas. And that just because someone thinks differently from yourself, it doesn't mean they're wrong. It means you should try and be open to that. And either you change your mind or you adapt your idea or it makes you more sure of your own idea. The children were amazing and I could see how this really affected their thinking and how they applied this in play and how we apply this in their learning in all different kinds of situations.

Kathy Brodie: So that is a true life skill you're giving them there. That's not just teaching them a lesson about colours or shapes. That's actually a proper embedded life skill that you're giving them.

So how long does it take to work with children like this, because this is a different way of working to what you'd expect to see in a lot of settings. How long does that take to get that system going, that approach embedded?

Suzanne Axelsson: I think you need to have a few years. I think you will notice changes in the beginning because it's like the honeymoon phase where you make changes, you become aware of your environment become aware of what you're doing. There's all these new things that you're adopting and seeing the child as competent and trying to let go of that power, but letting go of that power is really hard.

Changing the time is different because you giving everything much more time. While I think in many schools you have a very hard time agenda to follow - you need to do this, you need to do this, then this and then we're changing this and that this theme is happening. Valentine's Day is popping up.

It makes it very hard to be Reggio approach because there's a lot of these old traditions that keep having to be plopped in. And you haven't quite got the place where you questioning the validity of these traditions. And I'm not saying take away traditions because I think traditions are very important but we should be questioning why are we having these traditions? Have they any meaningful for the children? And Valentine's Day - I mean everyone notices it, all children notice it because its hearts and balloons and pinks and reds and all sorts all over town. So instead of celebrating Valentine's Day, I would ask the children what is love and would explore love. And then would create a piece of artwork based on their ideas of love.

Kathy Brodie: Even with very young children you'd ask them? That's a massive question.

Suzanne Axelsson: But mostly it was the parents in the beginning. And so because I had the children from when they were two until they were six, I was able to share with the children what they said their first years and each year develop their idea. They could see their own learning.

Kathy Brodie: I assume that you would share that with them and sit with the books and say look how you have developed and so on. I think that's so respectful to do that *with* children rather to then observe or make notes or take photos and kind of not even say to them oh I'm going to be doing this or is it all right if I do this that it feels much more respectful.

It's that co-construction - that coming together of ideas. So it's going to take a long time for practitioners to fully implement something like a Reggio Emilia approach. But if it is something that they would like to work towards, if it's something that they're aiming for, what would your one top tip be for practitioners or educators who were working in the Early Years?

Suzanne Axelsson: Reflection.

Kathy Brodie: Oh wow! All right. Okay. Unpack that a little bit for us.

Suzanne Axelsson: It will be taking the time to reflect on why we are doing what they're doing. Taking the time to reflect on each individual child taking the time to reflect on their own teaching.

Why am I doing this the way I am doing it?

I think without that reflection there's no point in doing the Reggio Emilia approach. It is about reflecting and about the processes, about yourself as a teacher, about the children as the group, about the learning, about which direction the group should be doing.

What is it they're doing at the moment? Is there interest about owls, for example? Is it about the anatomy of owls? or is it about that they're scared of owls? Or is it because they're scared of the dark and owls come out at night? To work out what it is about because then you understand what it is the children are *really* interested in, what they're really wanting to know. Then you can base everything - the maths, the science, the stories and everything can come up after the real interest.

Kathy Brodie: It will take a little more time for practitioners to really get into what the children are thinking and maybe the context where that has come from. And for me, it feels like there's going to be quite a lot more standing back and watching rather than diving in and doing – is that right?

Suzanne Axelsson: Absolutely. You are trying to make yourself invisible. You are the most successful in children's learning when their children can learn themselves. I'm invisible for the majority of the time, the children know I'm there and they can turn to me when they need me and I become visible when they need me or when I need them.

Sometimes the need can be that **I** see they have a need, and sometimes the children will learn how to ask for help because I think that is also important. I think a lot of people go through that, they say children say they have to be competent, have to do everything themselves. Now I would get the children and say – "it's fine to ask for help" to know where your limitations are. Maybe to ask a friend for help, rather than an adult because eventually these children will be adults. You want to have a doctor in the future who is fully capable of asking his doctor colleague for advice and help with something and not to be competent and survive on his own. I think I would have much more confidence in someone who can ask for help.

Kathy Brodie: I think that's a really, really great top tip - that the children can help themselves and within their peer group and we know any group of children you have some that are more confident and competent in some areas than others. And for children to recognize that in their own peer group is really nice.

I'm just thinking that's going to probably support their emotional development, as well, if somebody recognizes them as being the more knowledgeable other.

Suzanne Axelsson: Taking care of each other. When the children fall over, I mean, I'm always there, I always see. If it's a big fall or a big hurt I'm there, I'm on the spot. But when there's a smaller fall, instead of me rushing there and the children relying on the adults to help the child, I make sure that the children go over and ask "What do you need? How can I help him now?"

I've got an absolutely amazing photo series of children - the whole group - running over to a friend that's fallen over. They pick him up. They check their knees, check how they are, they hug them they ask them how can I help, they move them to a bench. They sit down for a while say "We can play again when you are ready to play". Modelling exactly the same things that I had done with them when we were younger and when they still needed adult help. But it was amazing they could do it themselves, because I believed that they could do it. I knew it could if I gave them the space the I made myself invisible.

Kathy Brodie: Such a lovely example! That's so nice and you know I think that I would be rushing in myself - it wouldn't occur to me to have the other children helping each other, so I think that's a lovely scenario.

Suzanne Axelsson: It's the hardest thing you do. You literally put your hands in your pockets when you're standing, or you sitting on your hands. You really really want to go over and help. And yes, definitely the first time you feel like you got your heart in your throat the majority of the time.

Sometimes they might come and say they're bleeding. We need a plaster and we'll go over and help them. But the same with climbing frames the children help each other. Rather than me lifting them on they're lifting each other up because they are empowered. They realize that they don't have to depend on an adult to fix their problems. They can be resourceful themselves and fix an awful lot more than what they have been given the time and the belief that they can do.

Kathy Brodie: I think again that's another fantastic life skill. You know that that resilience and all that that sort of goes with that package is just amazing I just think that's wow! and I'd love to see that piece of video as well because it sounds really good.

Now I know that you do have a blog and you have a Facebook and your blog is 'Interaction Imagination'. And I know I'm always on your Facebook, I spent a lot of time scrolling through the discussions with there's always a new picture or a new provocation on there.

You have the double whammy of both being Scandinavian and Reggio Emilia inspired and of course with your work in Palestine as well now, that's going to start to seep through as well. There are some lovely pictures from Palestine on there at the moment out there from your previous visit. So that's definitely worth going to.

Suzanne it is always a pleasure to sit and chat with you. Thank you so so much for sharing your expertise with us today. Just loads of things to go away and think about there. So thank you very much indeed for joining us on the Early Years.

Suzanne Axelsson: Thank you for having me.

CHAPTER 13

PRACTITIONER'S OWN WELL-BEING AND MINDFULNESS

Sonia Mainstone-Cotton

Kathy Brodie: I am absolutely thrilled to be joined by Sonia Mainstone-Cotton. Sonia is an early trainer and nurture consultant. She specializes in listening to children and promoting children's and staff wellbeing and has written the book 'Promoting Young Children's Emotional Health and Well-being: A Practical Guide for professionals and parents'. She's currently writing a follow up book on the emotional wellbeing of Early Years staff which is really exciting. I can't wait to see that. So welcome to the Early Years Web Summit Sonia Mainstone-Cotton.

Sonia Mainstone-Cotton: Thank you.

Kathy Brodie: First what I'd like to start with is the rationale for your book. Why did you decide to write about the emotional health and well-being? And how does this link to being a nurture consultant?

Sonia Mainstone-Cotton: I'm a nurture consultant, I work for a local organization. A nurture consultant for me means working with four year olds who are finding the transition into school really tricky. I'm self-employed doing that role and as a way of trying to understand what I was seeing and reflect on my practice and what I was observing, I started writing a blog. And that got picked up by Jessica Kingsley publishers and from that they asked me whether I would write something about emotional well-being promoting well-being. Because one of the things that kept coming up through my writing and from what I was seeing was these children have really poor well-being.

They're not feeling good about themselves.

They don't feel that they're special.

They don't feel safe.

And if those things aren't in place in Early Years then that doesn't give them a good start in life. And that kind of got me thinking around well-being and how important it is. And so often we hear about well-being with teenagers, we hear about well-being with adults, but particularly teenagers and mental health issues. We don't often hear about well-being with four year olds and within Early Years and Early Years is my passion. I felt that we needed to get it right. If we can get it right there, and that makes such an impact on the rest of life.

Kathy Brodie: I think that's a really critical thing, that by the time they get to teenage the golden opportunity is gone. It's catching it in the Early Years. I know when I've spoken to people about emotional well-being of very young children, they've kind of said to me but they're four! Why haven't they got that well-being? What sort of things might children not feel good about themselves where might their wellbeing be falling down?

Sonia Mainstone-Cotton: I think if things at home are quite difficult. I think if parents are stressed or distressed. If parents are finding parenting quite hard and that will have a knock on effect on the children. I think sometimes it's about children not spending lots of time with her parents and that be really difficult. So there are many, many different reasons - if parents have got ill health, if poverty is an issue and they're finding life difficult financially and they're worried - a lot these sorts of things, children can pick up on.

We know children are sponges and they will pick up on what's going on around them and that will have an impact on how they are and how they are feeling.

Kathy Brodie: Being in that environment, even if they're not having to pay the bills themselves, they can they pick up on that environment. And I think sometimes even if you're in a setting maybe if they know there's something not quite right in a setting they can pick up on practitioners wellbeing as well.

Sonia Mainstone-Cotton: Absolutely. So one of the chapters in the book that I wrote was on adult well-being. I think that's probably the most important chapter actually of that initial book, because I feel what I was beginning to see was, if the adults who were looking after the children aren't in a good place themselves, then that's very difficult for those children - and for them to be able to enhance the well-being of those children. It led to that whole thing of us as adults having good wellbeing and how important that is to be in a good place.

Kathy Brodie: Absolutely. I'm assuming that's the rationale for your follow on book, the emotional well-being of staff. So can you just expand on that little bit and what you're going to be discussing in that book.

Sonia Mainstone-Cotton: So that becomes looking at the different types of wellbeing and what we can do. So it's a practical guide, my writing is very practical, it gives lots of ideas about what you can do, what you could try. I'll be looking at physical well-being - say the food we eat, what we drink, what rest we take, what relaxation we have, how are we connecting with other people. How are we joining in with others and spiritual well-being.

Looking at connectedness with other people but maybe yoga and mindfulness. We often think about spirituality as in a religious group, and it might be that for some people, but for others it's that whole sense of mindfulness. It's yoga those sorts of things that come into that. And looking at how we can help ourselves and giving some very simple - because it's not rocket science really and it really isn't particularly complicated - but sometimes we just need to stop and have that reminder:

How are you doing there?

Are you eating?

Are you eating breakfast?

Are you taking a lunch break?

It's those sorts of things which are really crucial.

Kathy Brodie: That's only getting worse is it? As the Early Years sector expands as there's less money and things like having a full lunch break - those are things where it's going to get cut isn't it?

Sonia Mainstone-Cotton: It is! It's one of the questions I ask. There's a chapter in there for managers and one of the actions for managers is

Do your staff have a staff room?

Is it a room where your staff can feel that they can relax? Can they eat lunch their lunch in there?

Can they make themselves a drink?

Are there some comfy chairs?

Because often, and particularly in Early Years settings, the staff room is often the dumping ground and the room where small groups happen. You can't necessarily have your lunch break in that. And I know in some settings that's really hard. If you're a small setting, in a church hall, that's really difficult. And then you need to think a bit more creatively - how can you do that.

But actually having a breakout space I think is really important. So my book is wanting to explore what can managers do for staff and I'll be offering some ideas, but also, as staff what can we do for ourselves. How can *we* take some responsibility? So there are things that we can do and it just kind of offering some thoughts around that.

Kathy Brodie: I just think that's so needed at the moment and that obviously is linked very closely to the children's well-being as well doesn't it. Why do you think that this is becoming so important at the moment?

Sonia Mainstone-Cotton: I think there are a growing number of pressures. So I've worked in the Early Years field for over 25 years. And I think there is a growing amount of pressure on staff, on adults. And we know as in running settings that there are greater expectations on staff of things that need to be able to do things they need to move to.

There was research done which was brought out by Nursery World magazine at the end of 2015, where 59 per cent of Early Years staff said they were considering quitting the job due to high levels of stress and over workload. I think that definitely contributes that's something to do with it.

I did my own research a few weeks ago with staff who worked with children. So not just Early Years but across the sectors. And I interviewed 85 people. And the big things that were coming out was workload - the increasing workload. Still the paperwork demands are huge. They feel that they don't have necessarily the time to give the children that they used to give.

That's really difficult because I can't change that. I can't change people's workloads, I can't change government targets. But I think I can help people do practical things. What can we do and what will help us.

I think the other thing we're seeing and I'm seeing through my nurture work is there are a greater number of children that we're working with have higher emotional needs. So a greater number of children we're working with have behavioural issues that come out of their emotional needs.

I personally think there's something about the cutbacks that we've seen over the last five, seven years is beginning to have a trickle down effect, and we now see that in some of the families that we're working with.

If you're working with a really challenging child or children that has an impact on you. And how do you deal with that. So that's why I particularly became interested in this because the children that I work with are very challenging children and I support staff in how they work with those children. And I have noticed over the years how important it is that those Teaching Assistants (TAs) or those nursery staff are feeling good, those teachers are feeling good and calm. That enables the child to feel calm - but if they're feeling stressed and anxious then the children can pick up on.

Kathy Brodie: And you say TAs as well, so that's in schools as well as in Early Years settings. I think sometimes because Early Years settings are private businesses, there's an additional financial stress - you've got to balance the books or you have no business. And we sometimes we think that schools, where they don't have to do that, so they're in a much better place. But they presumably have workloads.

Sonia Mainstone-Cotton: They have to balance the books. You know they have limited money. It's very difficult to maybe allocate a full time TA because they may not have the budget for that.

Kathy Brodie: So we're getting the double whammy there are we were getting more children who have got emotional needs and staff who have less time to deal with that. Do you see that continuing into the future?

Sonia Mainstone-Cotton: Yes I do sadly. I'm not really seeing anything changing at the moment. And other colleagues are saying similar things. You know there was a concern about growing need and it needs financing. Money is quite important in putting those children and that key person approach in schools and having children working with somebody that they trust and need to meet their needs.

It's really important and it's not to say that schools aren't doing a good job because they're doing an amazing job - it's very hard you know. Very hard.

Kathy Brodie: Oh absolutely and I think sometimes it's those people that don't shout up because some of the time they just don't have the time or the energy to do that as well. They're just as you say just going under.

So that's sort of a fairly bleak picture we've painted there. What sort of things can we do? What practical strategies can we do to make that situation better to improve the lives of our children?

Sonia Mainstone-Cotton: So I think when it comes to thinking about the staff and what they can do, practical things they can do are: Thinking about their day, what they put in place - so are they eating in the way that we talk about children need to be eating - really well? We're great at encouraging healthy eating in children. Do we do it for ourselves? So we talk about the importance of children having breakfast. Actually do we have breakfast ourselves?

So one really easy example is - I used to work for a children's charity and in our team we had a kitchen in our office. We all worked in an office and went out in and out from the office. And often we would arrive quite fraught. Often hadn't had breakfast, we'd been doing school runs and you know getting out in the morning and it's difficult and fraught. So we had breakfast in our office. Our manager always had bread and butter or you know spreads, and we would have toast and other people would bring cereals and we would share that. We would often start the day by having breakfast and coffee, which was such a brilliant start to the day because it meant we were connecting with people which is really important.

The message from the manager was "I know your beginning of the day is fraught you need to eat before you can move on". Very, very simple.

So, in our staff rooms could you have some breakfast things? Are those things available? And lunch breaks we've talked about - I think that's really important. Drinking well, so drinking water those practical things. If you are dehydrated you're very tired. You can be very tired, it can make you quite grouchy you know. Do you have do your staff have water on tap? Are they able to drink throughout the day? Do they have water bottles around that they're able to access? So very simple things.

Something that I'm regularly saying - since I mostly worked with TAs and teachers in reception classes - at the end of our session is "what are you doing tonight that makes you feel good? What are you doing on the weekends? It's been a really stressful day today, so what are you going to do to look after yourself?

When I first start working with staff in September they always looked slightly puzzled - a bit what do you mean? By January they've got completely used to it - OK, this is what she's going to say and it's different for different people. So one TA I worked with she would finish her school day go home and walk the dog and by walking the dog it enabled her to get out of her head what happened during that day.

Another member of staff said, I exercise that's what does it for me. I get home and I exercise and by doing that it helps me to offload what's happened. And that's really important. I think that being able to offload.

Another really simple tool that I do - as I go from school to school during the day - so I come out of one school see each child, move on to another school - and I have hand cream in my car and if it's been a particularly stressful session for whatever reason, I'll get into the car and put some hand cream on. Just that gentle nurturing, that rubbing my hand cream into my hands. It lets me let go of the child I've seen and it just nurturing myself, it's giving myself some compassion, enabling me to go "It's OK. It's all right". I can move on.

Kathy Brodie: I love this. And that's so simple as you say that's so easy.

Sonia Mainstone-Cotton: Yeah really simple.

Kathy Brodie: I know that you talk and you write a lot about mindfulness. Can you tell us a bit about what that is please?

Sonia Mainstone-Cotton: Okay, so mindfulness. It's a very old ancient tradition. Mindfulness links back to Buddhist practice, old Christian practice of meditation of stopping and noticing but mindfulness practice now often doesn't use those Buddhist practice or to have to be a Buddhist or Christian to use it. It's about stopping and noticing.

You can use some mindfulness meditation. There are some online that you can download and listen to, which is just about stopping and breathing. You're noticing your breath. And I think when you talk about meditation often people think meditation is about emptying your mind.

Where mindfulness practice talks about - your mind will be full of things and that's fine, but it's about noticing the breath, it's noticing how you breathe and what impact that it has on your body. If we breathe properly, if we breathe deeply and fully then that's much better for your body. It's kind of allowing the oxygen to move round through the blood. Its much better, it's a much healthier way to be.

So mindful practice is about partly noticing and being in the moment. A good example of that is when we eat. We eat really quickly often and don't necessarily notice what you've eaten. Really lovely mindful practice is to have, say, a piece of chocolate or a blueberry. And you look at it and you notice and you think about how it's going to taste and you smell it. And then it's in your mouth and you hold it in your mouth for a moment and then you finally eat it and you're noticing those feelings how does it taste in your mouth. Is it what I thought it would be? Its that mindful moment. And I use mindfulness a lot.

I talk about mindfulness a lot with the staff I work with, about they could use mindful breathing techniques you could use every day. You come back at the end of the day and you're feeling quite agitated, its a good way of just getting yourself into a good place.

I tend to use mindfulness for me first thing in the morning before I go on a visit, I know it's going to be a hard one. And so this morning I had quite a difficult meeting to attend. So I just did a 10 minute mindfulness, just calming myself getting myself in a good place before I was moving on.

You can do it with the children as well. So with older children we talk about mindful breathing. You hold up your hands and you take a breath and you * tracing round the fingers of an outstretched hand * put your finger up, your finger and down round your thumb. You breathe in, you breathe out, you breathe in, breath out.

That's really easy practice. So I have reception class teachers that use that with children. You can use that with nursery children. Or using snow globes. Get a child to shake a snow globe. Or make a bottle is a similar idea - we get our glitter and water in a bottle. Get children to shake it and notice all those glitter shakes about and you say to children sometimes when we're feeling agitated or cross your feelings are like that. Then watch that glitter. Slow down. And that's a good mindful moment to do with children.

Kathy Brodie: Wow that's a really powerful images.

Sonia Mainstone-Cotton: And when you talk about it with children and staff around are going. "Oh Yeah that's great" It's just really simple tools. Often saying to staff, if you're feeling really stressed do the finger breathing you know just have a moment where you're doing finger breathing and just bring yourself down, bring yourself back to that place.

Kathy Brodie: And I'm guessing that's going to vary from person to person. Some people might latched on to other different areas of mindfulness minds.

Sonia Mainstone-Cotton: You know different things different things work for different people but it's about it's about giving people those tools I think. In our local authority, lots of schools now are delivering Mindfulness in Schools. Lots of staff are being trained in mindfulness. It's not quite reached the Early Years sector, it's beginning to kind of drip through. I know some settings that have paid for staff to go on mindfulness training and some people use those meditations every day. Some people will just use other moments, so that mindfulness noticing is something that works for them. So it's finding something that works.

Other people use yoga, so a lot of Early Years settings are introducing yoga to children. Having teachers come in and do yoga with nursery children and again the staff are using that and finding ways that that helps them very similar.

Kathy Brodie: I've seen a lot of the baby yoga going on but I've always viewed it from the point of view of the benefit for the children, but it hadn't occurred to me, of course that the practitioners are there as well. So they're benefiting as well.

Sonia Mainstone-Cotton: If they are joining in and using it.

Kathy Brodie: I just think that's so fascinating. That takes nothing really in the way of resources, that's not going to cost any money. But what a difference that is going to make if you come after a stressful morning. You've had a bit of a lunch break. You've got to go back out into the room. Just shake that snow globe. And just watch the glitter go down. And now you're ready to go out.

That can be very very powerful here. I'd love to do that with the children as well and see what they're like, especially those wet play days when they're all over the place.

So that's really a useful strategy. Thank you so much for those. I just want to return back to your book: Promoting Young Children's Emotional Health and Well-being. Is there anything else that we can do specifically for children to support their well-being in our settings?

Sonia Mainstone-Cotton: I think it's looking at the whole. And so the outdoor play is really is really essential I think. It's no surprise that the well-being of children when it's measured is much better in Scandinavian countries than it is here. And I think in Scandinavian countries what you see is children spend a lot of time outside. We know that forest school and outdoor play is really really important. And I think that's really important. You know how do you view playing outdoors in your setting. Do you view it as a way for children to let off steam? Do you view it as a way for children to really thrive and discover? All those kind of things - that awe and wonder. I think that's really important.

I think giving children stillness. I think introducing and 'unrushing' the agenda is important and again that's a very Scandinavian practice. I was on a study tour in Denmark a few years ago at a kindergarten in the woods and they spend every day in the woods and time in the woods.

There was one moment that really stood out for me - there was one little girl. She was about four or five (because they don't go to school until they're seven) and she was lying on a water trough. And it was a beautiful sunny day and she was lying in the sunshine, just on her back, looking up and she was there for about 20 minutes. She wasn't asleep. She was just enjoying that moment. I took a photograph of her and that's really stayed with me.

The question that it made me ask was - how often do we allow children time to just be? Do we allow children that time to just stop and relax and just be? Or are we so often moving them on from the next things to the next thing.

One of the things I explored in that chapter is around we, as adults talk about being busy all the time. So often you'll say to somebody how busy are you. But often we do that for children as well, I know lots of children who were doing lots of clubs after school and one girl who was seven and she went to two or three different after school clubs every day and then things on the weekend. And that's not unusual anymore I think particularly with middle class parents that's a really common thing.

So, are we allowing children time to rest, to relax to daydream? That's what the little girl was doing - she was lying there and just daydreaming. There's an argument that some of our most creative moments are when we stop and when we daydream and that's what I think we need to allow children to do. I don't think we talk about that. I don't think that's something that really gets discussed.

Kathy Brodie: Absolutely not. When you go to a Pinterest or if you're looking at routines it's about what *more* can we give them what extra activity can we squeeze in here. You never see anything that says this is a great time for them just to sit and be. Just go and find a nice comfy cushion and just sit and be for a moment. Also I've never seen that on planning yet. Maybe we should maybe we should always plan that in some way.

Now, that's not going to take any resources at all, that's very cheap, it's very easy to do, even if it is you're just seeing that a child's maybe just having a little bit of a quiet moment, not going interrupting them and saying "oh do you want to come and join me". Not doing anything just to allow them that bit of time maybe? And that's such an easy sort of thing that you can do with children, isn't it? That is absolutely fascinating mindfulness.

I have done a little bit of reading of yours on mindfulness, but I shall be definitely be going back and having a look at some more strategies for me. I think that's a that's very powerful for practitioners definitely.

Thank you so so much Sonia and your book is published by Jessica Kingsley and you can get it obviously by using bookstores or via Amazon if you want to get that. And just remind me of your website address www.Soniamainstone-cotton.com

Kathy Brodie: Lovely. Nice and easy. We like those. And there'll be a link on the website too on the summit website to your website there as well.

Sonia Mainstone-Cotton: Absolute pleasure.

CHAPTER 14

THE PRACTICAL BENEFITS OF NEUROSCIENCE IN CHILDREN'S PSED – BEING BRAIN BUILDERS

Mine Conkbayir

Kathy Brodie: I am absolutely thrilled to be joined by Mine Conkbayir. Mine is the training and development director and associate at NEYTCO, the membership organization for trainers, consultants and researchers in early childhood education. She was the acting head of the Centre for Research learning development at the London Early Years Foundation (LEYF) where she lectured on the Early Childhood Studies degree program. She writes extensively on subjects concerning the changes in the childcare sector and is also the author of 'Early Childhood Theories and Contemporary Issues.'

She has a second book out at the moment, which is 'Early Childhood and Neuroscience Theory: research and implications for practice.' And that has just been published by Bloomsbury.

Mine is currently studying for her PhD in Early Childhood Education and neuroscience in order to further her extensive work in the complex and challenging arena of neuroscience, but more importantly its potential use in early childhood policy and practice. A very warm welcome to the summit, Mine Conkbayir.

Mine Conkbayir: Thank you very much Kathy. I am very, very honoured to be part of this podcast.

Kathy Brodie: I can't wait to hear what you have to say about neuroscience because it's a really growing area isn't it? But starting with some of your research and the things that you've found. Could you just explain to me what we mean by neuroscience, what exactly is neuroscience?

Mine Conkbayir: Okay, the dull bit first! Neuroscience is the scientific study of the nervous system, so broadly speaking that is: the central nervous system, which is the brain and the spinal cord, and the peripheral nervous system, which is all the nerves and the ganglia which are bundles of nerve cells connected by synapses outside of the brain and the spinal cord.

So, in relation to children's learning and development, neuroscience provides us with abundant evidence concerning how the brain develops and grows and how environmental factors like relationships, attachments, and early experiences literally shape or sculpt early brain development. So every experience that the infant has, results in new neural pathway, that's a brain cell connection, being made.

The brain is greatly 'experience expectant' and 'experience dependent' - it needs those experiences in order to grow. And repetition of these experiences get laid down as neural pathway, like motorways in our brain, which become further strengthened the more exposure the child has.

Consider *your* skills and strengths - you had to practice that over and over again to gain your mastery. This applies to children, but all the more so because, as per Piaget's theory, they're in that sensorimotor phase, so they do need hands on experiences in order to learn to build mastery through touch, testing, investigating, exploration and trial and error until they find the answer that they need. The correct answer for them.

So typically a baby is born with at 86 billion neurones, which I think is staggering. But that doesn't mean that it's job done, because our brains are built over time. So whenever I work with practitioners, be it level three, foundation degree, students or parents I tell them that we are all 'brain builders' and this is crucial for two reasons:

Firstly, poverty of affection, positive experiences, lack of quality interactions and resources can result in these neural pathways from not being formed, as the stimuli that the brain needs are either missing - or not happening consistently enough for those neural connections to be formed and embedded. Those motorways are not done, they're not made.

Secondly, negative experiences like chronic maltreatment, abuse, neglect and chronic toxic stress cause the brain to wire - that is to form neural connections - in response to these negative experiences. So this is bad news on so many levels. Physiologically the infant's brain will be telling or signalling to his body that he's in danger. So they'll be hypersensitive to perceived dangers that might not be there but their bodies are under that kind of stress all the time. So, that would be the child who's generally anxious, fretful, finding it difficult to trust and ultimately to learn and thrive. And that's not just in nursery. But later on at school and of course well into adulthood.

Neuroscience also confirms that there exists 'sensitive' periods for learning and development. The brain is at its most plastic and that means open to learning from birth to five years. There's strong evidence for the fundamental importance for the first thousand and one critical days - conception to two years and there's a lot of brilliant work being done by Claire Reese and her colleagues into that and we'll come onto that again later.

Kathy Brodie: So babies are born with all the potential. It's not only use it and lose it, which is what we think about reinforcement.

But also you've got to form those things in the first place through positive experiences, through hands on things and that can also be a negative. So those babies have got all that potential. It depends on what we do then. So, with that in mind then it, depends on what happens to a baby once they're born and all those experiences as you say from conception really within the first 1001 days. How does that effect emotional development?

Mine Conkbayir: Emotional development and wellbeing and

early brain development are inextricably linked. The babies are programmed for socialization, they expect and need love in order to thrive. If we think about Ericson's first stage of psychosocial development from birth to a year that child is either trust or mistrust - they're in that stage aren't they?

Their understanding is very quickly - is this world warm, safe, am I happy, do I feel okay to explore and cry and get my needs met? Or is it a harsher landscape? Is it cold and hostile where I'm not allowed to make my voice heard? They know that very quickly.

If a baby or a child enjoys positive, respectful, caring and supportive relationships, they feel calm, secure, confident and happy. This literally frees up key brain regions to learn as the brain's emotional centre - which is the amygdala I'll mention that again a bit later on - isn't signalling to other brain regions and the body that she's in danger.

So the prefrontal cortex, which is this front part the large part brain, can function at its full potential. The prefrontal cortex is our control centre for higher order skills. When we talk about school readiness, we're talking about all of those skills that reside in the prefrontal cortex. Your reading, your planning, your problems solving. Crucially the ability to self-regulate emotions, to concentrate, to use working memory and to learn.

Leading on from this a healthy brain, as I like to call, it is one which gets enough of the right fuels it needs to ensure its healthy growth and development. So it sounds basic, but when you have so much of this exciting new science showing us what happens when children take enough exercise, when they are stimulated enough, when there's a lot of physical activity, this releases the happy hormone as we call it serotonin and dopamine. Physical activity actually enhances synaptogenesis - that simply means the creations of neurones - new brain cells.

This coupled with a healthy diet, with as much natural wholefoods as possible. My biggest bugbear at the moment is tech device use - by both parental and child. You know when that's to a minimum or when it's supervised and it's not hours on end, that with abundant love and nurturing and respectful relationships all these factors sculpt 'healthy' brains.

Kathy Brodie: So when you're talking about a healthy brain you're talking about the biological healthy brain as well as an emotionally healthy brain as well.

Mine Conkbayir: Absolutely, because they're so tightly linked. You know if we don't have happy, healthy children that feel safe enough we underestimate it. But children they fall down, they cry or you know their friends not being very nice, but they get chastised by their parents for showing an emotion when they're in pain - that's not healthy and that's not helpful to that child. It's not teaching them how to accept their feelings and how to overcome them. It's saying "no, you're wrong for feeling sad". Actually they're not. And they need our help.

Their brains are still developing up to the age of 25. Our brains are not set. Though the brain grows it develops throughout life but it's less open and malleable and that's why we call this the sensitive period from birth to five.

Kathy Brodie: I think that sort of visual image of a plasticity is very good because it is it's forming and reforming and making those connections according to the experiences that you have and children have very strong emotions and they can be very overwhelming. Sometimes as adults we get overwhelmed!

Mine Conkbayir: Absolutely and I think we talk about a plastic brain. No more is it this plastic when you are two years old, synaptogenesis - that big plurification of new synapses and brain cells - happens most at two years, not 15 years not at 20 years old so there is a lot of brilliant work to be done with our youngest.

I know it's the example that's used all too often but we must never forget it. The tragic case of the Romanian orphans. A few of those were lucky enough to be fostered into loving American and English families and they develop the skills that they were not able to develop early on in life. But it still isn't the same. There are still some neural behavioural scars, as I call them, because it wasn't done in that optimum time frame.

Kathy Brodie: And that's quite brief isn't it when you think - 0 to two and everything else that's going on during that time the physical development, it's a biological need as well. There's an awful lot of other things going on in there as well as the emotional environment isn't there?

Mine Conkbayir: Absolutely, but that's why I like to say it's from conception because anything that pregnant mum does - you know the stress levels, is it chronic? Is there domestic violence?

I know some of those examples were extreme and I'd like to be honest with you at this point. My childhood wasn't fantastic. I had a wonderful mum, unconditional love but it was chaotic. My brain and body were cranked on permanently high for stress. I was wired for it. I'd look for it when it wasn't there and when there wasn't a danger I'd be like "Oh, what's going on?" and then it would erupt and I'd be like "Yeah, I'm feeling excited over what's going - oh this is wrong".

I'm an adult, I am a mum and I realize oh dear, oh very dear, to my parents and what they put us all through, because now I am that adult, I do get depressed periods at length, I am anxious and I am hypersensitive to what I think of as threats in my environment. I know for a fact that's from my experience and what I witnessed as a child.

I think if kids have access to accessible friendly non patronizing information about the choices they make or certain behaviours they have especially pregnant women then they can be encouraged and supported to make different choices for themselves and for the benefit of their unborn child.

Kathy Brodie: Thank you for sharing that very personal experience with us. Is that the general reaction to stressful or highly emotionally charged circumstances? Would you expect to see that in a lot of children out there that constantly you know "oh it's all gone quiet. I know there's going to be a problem in a minute". Do you think that would be typical?

Mine Conkbayir: Very typical Kathy, because there's a close link in the limbic system between emotions and memories. So primarily because the limbic system contains the brain's emotional centre, which I mentioned earlier on, the amygdala (or amygdali because there's more than one). So there's two of them and they are small almond like structures deep in the brain and they are responsible for coordinating behavioural responses to emotional stimuli in the environment. So that, with the hippocampus (which is like a tiny seahorse structure) deep in the brain that's related to fear and anxiety is a key player in the formation of memories.

To contextualize this, a child who is conditioned by the caregiving in those Early Years will grow up understanding that "oh okay I'm in danger". So their amgydala will be on high alert almost constantly - in flight or fight mode. Basically that becomes activated then they're rendered unable to learn, because their amgydala, the limbic system with pathways to the prefrontal cortex, hijacks its regular functioning. So like I mentioned earlier the prefrontal cortex is all about our school readiness, all those key qualities and skills we need to enable us to learn. That doesn't happen because it gets skipped, because the amygdala goes "Alert!

Help! Danger! Danger!" We call that The amygdala hijack and I talk at length about this in my book and it's a term that Daniel Goldman, the guru of emotional intelligence has coined.

It's a very real thing in stressful situations. Chronic toxic stress is hazardous to healthy brain development. We know this first hand when we're feeling anxious, under pressure, fretful, sad, we're literally not in the right frame of mind to learn. All the more so young children, who are dependent on us and they need the right modelling and the right support in order to thrive.

But that said it's not all doom and gloom. A bit of stress is actually useful. Evolution tells us that it gives us the 'get up and go' in the mornings and it protects us from danger. And this is due to the stress hormone called cortisol. It peaks in the mornings and then it ebbs in the evenings because we're getting ready to go to bed and everything's calm. But you know during flight or fight, especially it's when a child is continually exposed to uncaring harsh responses, that there are issues at home, that cortisol becomes set on high - volume dial that's permanently set at maximum - I call it 'catastrophic cortisol' because a stressed up child can not thrive.

Kathy Brodie: So that sort of that stress, that constant fight or flight, that's kind of a road block then. If we are using the highway analogy - that's a road block to get into higher functioning and with some children there's always things going on at home. But on occasion, there might be the gerbil might die or something that's going to be very sad.

Mine Conkbayir: So a healthy normal stress, they will be supported through dealing with, but it's when they have no control or they are at the receiving end of this abuse or this maltreatment or they're witnessing things they simply shouldn't be witnessing. They cannot be expected to keep all of that inside and go to nursery in the morning and go and learn your numbers or your alphabet. It's just not going to happen and how mean and uncaring of us to think that that can happen effectively. That's massive pressure, massive stress on that child just it's not fair.

Kathy Brodie: Sometimes, of course, we just don't know that's what's going on at home, so things like domestic violence or maybe there's homelessness situation or just maybe chaotic lives, just not got any structure or routine or so on and that sort of thing can really affect them. But as far as the children are concerned, that's normal isn't it.

Mine Conkbayir: Absolutely. You don't realize it. Like I said earlier on, that was my norm, when there wasn't chaos I was thinking "oh what's going on here". That doesn't fit into my pattern of normal. And to this day, honestly, Kathy when I see happy partners with their children and it's all lovey, I find it always lovely. Like it doesn't quite fit my frame of normality because I didn't have it. And I remember growing up feeling so and so has a mum and they're really happy and laughing at home cause I didn't.

It affects you in different ways, but I've used it as a positive force to try and do something positive and make some changes that will help how our practitioners and our parents to understand.

Earlier on you just mentioned we don't necessarily know what's going on at home or you know what the circumstances are like, but our deep knowledge of child development and of that child as an individual should hopefully be enough for us to understand "ah okay something's not right here. I need to speak to someone".

Kathy Brodie: And to pick up maybe on those non-verbal things or maybe little things with mum.

Mine Conkbayir: Or things in role play, what they say, or behaviour to the adults or their responses to you at your invitation to play - are they fretful? Are they confident and if they're not, why? Just question a bit more.

Kathy Brodie: So it's just thinking that little bit further that little bit deeper and looking for those the wider picture really.

Mine Conkbayir: Absolutely and not to be afraid to act on something that they feel is wrong. A lot of trainee teachers say "Yeah, but I'm too scared to" And I'm like "no no no no no you don't be scared. You are the voicepiece for that child you have to speak up, you're that child's advocate".

Kathy Brodie: And that's that has got to be where our first responsibility comes isn't it you know the health of that child.

That moves us nicely on to some practical strategies and top tips for practitioners on how to support children's healthy brains so that they actually make all those connections and have all the good things going on in a setting.

Mine Conkbayir: If I'm repeating myself, I do apologize but again for practitioners to really realize what they are worth, what they mean to that child, and that they are a 'Brain Builder'. Everything they say, they do, how they respond to that child and they're playful, cues joining in in their play, the affirmation, the need for security contributes to brain development.

They really do need to give each child their best. So I'd like to say that 'connections outside, create connections inside'. By this I mean that their relationship with all children, their positive modelling, the rich language that they use, and their connection with that child and the environment creates new neural connections. I find that very, very exciting and powerful.

I've mentioned the sensitive period. Early Years practitioners work with children from birth to five years - the a sensitive period of brain growth and development - so I don't know how many viewers will remember that 80s film Johnny Number 5? It had a robot and he wants to learn more about his new world, which is planet Earth, and he zooms around everywhere picking up books and toys, movies saying "input, input. I need more input". That's our young children, that's what they're like. They're not passive little recipients waiting, you know like John Locke tabula rasa would have it. Let's construct knowledge, let's find out and we need to help them on that journey of exploration.

So Kathy I think more of your Sustained Shared Thinking needs to happen more consistently in our settings so that we give these young brains, which are so curious and thirsty for knowledge, the fuel they need to ensure their health, the growth and development.

Kathy Brodie: And we've already touched on it, but those practical experiences, the real life - the whole thing about, if you give a child a picture of an apple you're only going to get certain aspects of it but you give them a real life apple to taste, look, smell, All those are going to help.

Mine Conkbayir: Everything! the other day I bulk bought loads of porridge boxes and they came in a massive box. Delilah grabbed the box out of my hands (that's my daughter) and she dived in - "Mum, what are we going to make?" And I said could make a boat, we've got two long wooden sticks or a canoe and she's like, no lets make a car. So you know we cut out a paper plate, made the steering wheel, drew the wheels. She drew a radio on it, tinsel on the sides. It's fantastic!

But it's our questioning with that child – it's as if we are with friends, we are genuinely engaged. So why don't we give our children that? Why is it different? Why do some adults find it a chore to actually have a conversation with our youngest babies especially giving babies that eye contact, the nods, the smiles, the curiosity, the leading questions, the probing, setting of tiny problems in a bigger question because they have the ability to find those answers and they need to be given the opportunity to do so. And that's our job. That's where we come in.

Kathy Brodie: Absolutely. I think even setting little challenges rather than presenting things. "Oh this is what we're going to do today and this is how you're going to do it". Challenge them, make children think about it and that is from babies and there's some lovely clips on YouTube, where you have a baby lying on a rug and there's a toy just out of reach and she's reaching and reaching for it.

Mine Conkbayir: That object permanence that comes in. What do you think will happen if we...? I really dislike it - and I know they do it as a joke - but some adult bemoan that it's always: "Why?" "what if? what if? what if?". What I'm saying is turn it on its head. *We* need to ask those questions Why? Why? or what if this? what if that? because children love it. They want to be stretched.

Kathy Brodie: Yeah absolutely. And we know that does make those good brain connections.

Mine Conkbayir: Absolutely Kathy, those types of motorways are being formed.

Kathy Brodie: I'm interested that you mentioned school readiness, when you were talking about the higher functions and so on. A lot of things that we think about school readiness are things like lining up, making sure you can write your name, all those things but in fact you're talking about a very different sort of school readiness there aren't you?

Mine Conkbayir: Well I think the ability to regulate one's emotions starts early on in childhood. The ability to socialize, to understand others, to have empathy, all these things I think need to be in place before a child can be expected to be thrown into a new environment.

It's pretty daunting you know. It's a massive big school perhaps a uniform, different expectations, perhaps less friends there and you need to first know that a child's softer skills (I don't even like them being called softer skills) but those qualities of being able to calm yourself down or get along with others, you know yourself all of those things that adults really do need to help to sculpt in those Early Years if they're not there then that child cannot be expected to learn effectively.

You know, if they can't manage their own emotions, if they're feeling anxious or scared, if they're not supported to first feel calm, happy, secure then they will not go on to thrive in that school. So for me school readiness is a big issue, I think for a lot of practitioners out there right now actually. We need to focus on building our children up to be happy and confident before you need to go to school and you are expected to do ABC – it's not going to work that way. We have to flip it on its head.

Kathy Brodie: Oh absolutely. I think especially in the U.K. where they start so young as well, you got a much narrower window of opportunity there. It's really interesting to hear that's a biological process. I think sometimes we think about children they just kind of develop all by themselves. But we can affect that on a biological brain based level.

Mine Conkbayir: Massively! I once presented and I devised this spiral, it's like you know brain bonding and behaviour because they're all inextricably linked. Like I said earlier on, I think if a child is distressed and it's not eased by the adult, or it's exacerbated by the adult, that has immediate physiological effects. The heart's racing, the palms are sweaty, the stomach's in knots you know, they are very real.

To a young child or infant that's very overwhelming. If they're not able to be supported, to deal with these feelings and deal with uncomfortable emotions (because we all have to deal with uncomfortable emotions sometimes) then that will be an older child, teenager, adult that hasn't managed to fit into society as one would have expected them to, because everything else that came before wasn't quite right. It's like trying to put a big load of juicy cream and a cherry on top of the cake that wasn't quite well made with shaky foundations not the right ingredients.

So we do need to be more conversant with neuroscience and how it impacts us and our children on a daily basis I think Kathy. My simple point in all of this is for hundreds of years we've been taught about Vygotsky and Piaget in more recent theory Bronfenbrenner and Erickson many more of course and Bowlby to understand how children develop and how they behave and why. But now neuroscience is giving us scientific evidence for that. And I find that very exciting and almost it's urgent, now. We need to take it on board and we need to start utilizing it in ways that are practically meaningful.

Kathy Brodie: Oh absolutely I couldn't agree more. And as you say if we don't then there will be blocks to learning and it's as simple as that really isn't it.

Mine Conkbayir:. And another thing before I end up. But you know this thing of contemporary Childhood and I mentioned earlier about tech devices invading those Early Years and it's about excessive parental use more. That concerns me even more so than child use. But we have to move with the times. So ICT, lovely, many positive benefits, of course that's moving more into the early childhood curriculums in England.

Why isn't neuroscience being more used? I know some policies are coming around but you know they're slow and they're not enough. So hopefully in the next few years we will see that being built upon.

Kathy Brodie: Definitely, because the evidence is there isn't it. It is indisputable now. Its really interesting as to how we can use neuroscience in our practice and I know in your book Early Childhood and Neuroscience that is actually a lot of what you're talking about isn't it - how you can then use that knowledge in practice.

Mine Conkbayir: Absolutely. So here it is, nice and bright * holding up book * - My first one was neon pinks so I like to keep a trend!

Each chapter follows a similar format and I present the science by breaking it down immediately with real life case studies that have been provided by childhood trauma specialists, play therapists, nursery managers, Early Years practitioners and parents. I've put in a snippet by me as well as a parent to a bilingual four year old which makes a nice entertaining little giggly laugh.

There are questions for the practitioner to reflect on, to consolidate their understanding of what I've written about and then what it can mean in practice. I then put in Top Tips for practice based on the science that I presented. Chapter 3 talks a lot about the limbic system and its relation to emotions and learning which we discussed in this podcast.

I think it's very practical. I think I have managed to hit the notes that I intended to. Also recently I spoke at the Nursery World show which was held in London and a lot of the students and practitioners there, who watched us present based on this book as well as read the book, were giving a lot of positive comments saying that it made sense to them, they're definitely going to take it back to their settings and discuss it with their colleagues and managers.

I hope that with this work I helped to break down some of the barriers that have existed concerning neuroscience and Early Childhood Practice. I don't know whether I should say this, but I started out writing this book with a neuroscientist and it didn't end well. So I was left thinking "oh my goodness. Who am I to write a book about neuroscience?" He was supposed to fill in the theoretical background. And then I thought actually "no, I know enough, I can learn more. And I am going to write it" because his attitude was exactly that that we need to smash through and that it's elitist - it's for use in primary, secondary education but there is not much to tell Early Years practitioners! No, you're wrong. And we're going to prove you wrong actually. And this book I hope helps to chisel away at that barrier of those elitist beliefs which are incorrect. You know I think it's also quite patronizing because it forms that belief is that well so much of this is misconstrued.

Say, for example, Kathy you know there are two brain images - one of the shrivelled brain one of the healthier brain. So you use that as a correlation for abuse equals this and that's an extreme example, that was taken from a Romanian orphans survivor of neglect. And one of them is of a healthy brain. So they're basically saying you cannot extrapolate to that extent.

Well of course we can not and we will not. And you know they talk about misinformation and what I call 'neuro-nonsense' in my book, so things that are a little bit true but they get exaggerated so we get these neuro-myths, they will abound. The more we are not allowed access or made to believe that neuroscience doesn't have anything to tell us so we're going to wrap these nuggets and go "Oh yeah but that's true because so-and-so said it - that drink's really good for your brain"

I dispel all these myths in my book Kathy, I think in the first chapter actually, so the more we get to grips with this science the more we can interpret for ourselves and make the decision - Yes this is true. No this is not based on this evidence. But if you're closing those doors what are we expected to do? Actually I'm not going to mention the researcher's name, but more work is being done with Early Years practitioners and health visitors with neuroscientists to show that there is a big relationship. Of course, there's a big relationship. We know that anyway. But now you've got educational neuroscientists saying yes and here's the evidence which is what I've been moaning about for years, but didn't get listened to and ignored a lot of the time so for me to be able to write this book. And you know get it. Praised by an eminent neuroscientist actually means a lot to me and also Colwyn Trevarthen. So I am proud of it.

And I just want it to be practically useful. I want practitioners to be able to pick it up and go right. What does this mean? How can I use that in practice? I'm hoping that I've achieved that. We need to build on and get more informed policies concerning neuroscience out there and hopefully more consistent teaching of early brain development and neuroscience in our early childhood qualifications, which is what my PhD is exploring.

Kathy Brodie: Couldn't agree more, that we definitely need modules on neuroscience on Early Childhood Studies degree courses. That's really interesting that you've felt that you've not been listened to for quite a long time, because the evidence is out there - 1001 critical days you've already mentioned and there's a link on the website to that as well so we can click through and have a look on that that's finding more and more that the more we do the early the ages the better the outcomes.

Mine Conkbayir: I think it's like I said in that guest blog post for you - it's not rocket science but it is neuroscience and although a lot of people who say - it's common sense, love your children, play with them! But many parents for one reason or another find it very difficult. And it's about not judging them but enabling them to form that crucial loving relationship. with their child.

Kathy Brodie: And the knock on effects that it can have as well and how it can increase good outcomes for children. I think the book's absolutely amazing. It just blew me away. So I'm really pleased we've been able to talk a little bit about what's in there.

Thank you so much for joining us today. Its been absolutely amazing a thoroughly enjoyed it. I think the image of highways and having those blockages is really good for me. It's a visual learner. But I really like this idea of having a cake, unless the cake is right putting the cream and the cherry on top is a total waste of time. And I think that's a really strong image as well. But thank you so much for sharing all your fantastic expertise on that. Very best of luck with your PhD, Can't wait to read the outcomes of that and how that's going to affect our practice. Thank you so much indeed.

Mine Conkbayir: Thank you. Kathy it was a pleasure.

CHAPTER 15

USING THE LEUVEN SCALES TO IMPROVE OUR PRACTICE

Dr Sue Allingham

Kathy Brodie: I'm very excited to be joined by Dr. Sue Allingham. She's a consultant, author and trainer. And she's well-known through her writing for The Early Years Educator magazine, the EYE magazine that we all know, where she's also consultant editor. Sue's written the book 'Transitions in the Early Years: a practical guide to supporting children between Early Years settings and into Key Stage One'. And that's published by Practical Pre-school.

Supporting environmentally appropriate practices is one of Sue's particular interests. And Sue runs projects working with Year One teachers to create effective teaching and learning environments. She's been fully trained in using the Leuven scales for well-being and involvement, and this is the area that we're going to investigate today. Welcome to the Early Years Web Summit, Dr Sue Allingham.

Dr Sue Allingham: Thank you very much Kathy. It sounds really odd when people introduce me as Dr Sue Allingham - I sound like a medical practitioner! But thank you for that.

Kathy Brodie: You're very welcome and I shall refer to Sue now. So, the Leuven Scales - I love the Leuven Scales. I use them a lot when I do training and certainly when I'm teaching university. You talk about them and refer back to them a lot.

However, there may be people that I haven't come across the Leuven Scales before. So first of all can you just tell me a little bit about what they are.

Dr Sue Allingham: I think that's a really interesting point when you say that people have heard about the Leuven scales and in fact probably over the last couple of years the Leuven Scales have been bandied around as if there's something that everybody has heard of. Well they have now, but whether they actually understand what they really are is another question

About 10 maybe 12 years ago I first met Ferre Laevers, who was the person who first developed the idea of scales for well-being and involvement. And basically you have two sets of scales that work on a five point system. So you have the well-being scale and you have the involvement scales.

Now these are put into all sorts of assessment regimes these days, notably the type that you do on ipads, and also they're used in baseline assessments too. Professor Laevers realized that if you don't have a good sense of well-being that he refers to as feeling "like a fish in water", then actually your involvement in any kind of deep level learning isn't going to really happen.

We were talking a bit just now about our Internet and driving and things like that. We don't necessarily know what's going on with it and if we're very tense and the Internet goes wrong or the driving goes wrong and we don't understand why, our well-being is shot to pieces. Therefore, we can't get involved in understanding what's going wrong.

And if you watch young children, if they aren't feeling cared for and loved and understood then they're not going to be really listening to you when you try to teach them a new subject.

Really I suppose if you think about it, it's the Maslow's hierarchy isn't it? If we don't have our basic psychological needs met we're not going to fulfil our full self and develop self esteem. So Professor Ferre Laever's realized that you could actually sit down and monitor children's well-being. And I don't like the word grade or level, but effectively that's what it is, against five scale points and then depending on where that child is on the five points for well-being, you know how involved they're going to be in their learning. It's very much more complicated than that but that's it in a nutshell.

Kathy Brodie: So it's almost like a quick reference guide so rather than having to have a massive paragraph about 'this is what the child's doing', you can say well there were about midway on the scales or they're very high in their level of involvement. Its a really nice little shortcut way of condensing all that information. But as you say it's not as simple as that is it. There's a lot more that goes on behind all the scales.

Dr Sue Allingham: Yeah I mean you and I both know what we're talking about here. But for people who haven't had a background training on it's not quite so obvious. I mean for example I always say to people, you can't really do the involvement scales, unless you've looked at the well-being scale.

Kathy Brodie: Right. So you would start with the well-being scale.

Dr Sue Allingham: Always I would always start there. You might notice a child's not involved but I would probably guarantee that that's more to do with the fact that they haven't got an established well-being yet.

I mean we all have days where we're not involved in things don't we? We really can't find the flow to cope with it. Csikszentmihalyi isn't it, and we can't find our flow. We all have days like that. But if you've got a child who is consistently not involved in their learning then you would go straight to wellbeing and start unpicking that. But really from my point of view because PSED is my main interest and I've done a lot of work with Early Years and into Year One, as you said earlier I would always walk into any setting and look at how I feel about the wellbeing in there and it's not just about the children.

I always advocate for all of the well-being and involvement you can do with the adults as well. So if I'm ever doing any kind of be PSED training I always talk about whenever we say look at the child look at the adults as well.

Kathy Brodie: That's really interesting. Just thinking about settings I know where there is high level involvement, the adults are highly involved as well. You can't have a high level involvement of the children if the adults are sitting around doing nothing.

Dr Sue Allingham: No. And sadly that does happen in a lot of settings that I visit and also I think people don't put a lot of store in empathy sometimes. And if a member of the team is really stressed or something's gone wrong or there's tension in the team and I'm sure you've worked with teams where there's tension, as have I, that that rubs off on the children. You can't pretend it's not there. And so if you're not working with the well-being of the team you're not really working with the well-being of the children.

Kathy Brodie: So this is that whole holistic environment that's surrounding the child, from the moment they walk in as well isn't it. Not just during small group activities.

Dr Sue Allingham: Absolutely. It's the whole feeling of the room I do a lot of work around the emotional environment as well as the physical environment. You can't have one without the other.

Kathy Brodie: Yeah absolutely. Let me move on a little bit to the emotional environment as well. So that's a little bit about how we can use the Leuven scales to assess how on the five points we can kind of say this is where they are on those five points and starting off with the well-being.

So once we make that kind of assessment that's one way of using that assessment how can we use a Leuven scales to actually support emotional development in children?

Dr Sue Allingham: Well that's really really important part of the process and Ferre has what he calls the POM - Process Oriented Monitoring system. Because if you don't get the *process* right you can't get the monitoring right.

So he has what he calls the 10 action points for making your environment more emotionally friendly for the child to become involved. And actually in Early Years it's basic stuff that we know about the enabling environment. Having areas of interest, having the comfort areas, making sure there's enough room things like that, bringing in objects of interest that might be a bit different.

Some of the older books talk about bringing in magicians and things like that. Which is wonderful but you don't do it every day. When I picture a kind of real wellbeing involvement, I tend to think about Reggio type areas. Really comfortable, not all singing, all dancing, covered in laminates and coloured pictures and hanging things but it's a calming but very interesting and obviously emotionally stable, caring environment.

And so when we do work on the 10 action points for the children it's about appealing, one of the words in the 10 action points is how the areas and corners are 'appealing'. It's not about covering them with coloured numbers and letters and alphabets

Kathy Brodie: So it actually looks appealing for the children, not appealing for the teachers point that they want to put across.

Dr Sue Allingham: Exactly. And just keeping it real. People get very worried about how many letters and signs and things. And how do you keep your laminate pictures up on the walls outside and things. If you walked into a lovely garden it wouldn't have laminated pictures all over it would it.

Kathy Brodie: Absolutely. they certainly don't in the RHS gardens.

Dr Sue Allingham: That's a very valid point. So it's always checking of course as well that things are in good order, room awareness, environmental awareness. Is there enough paper? Is it good quality? It's basic stuff that actually we all know if we think about it but in the day to day running of a setting sometimes gets overlooked. Are things on the floor and the pencils are broken. Obvious stuff but we really need to remember it. Which is why, when you're doing Leuven work, you need to be thinking about the adults as well.

Kathy Brodie: So if you were going to do some training or if you were going into a setting as a consultant, is that how you would start? Would you start with the adults and look at where they are first and then go in with the children?

Dr Sue Allingham: Yeah. I've been in this sort of line of work for a long time in one way or another. But the first thing I do when I walk into any environment is register the feeling. Where are the adults? What are they doing? What are the interactions like? What are the children doing?

And then I look at so what is the environment like. Actually it could be a tatty as most dilapidated scout hut in the universe that the setting is having to use and it's not their fault it's like it. But it could be the best playgroup in the world.

Kathy Brodie: Yes, absolutely and I certainly I can think of several right now that have got the most lovely feeling when you come in and you are welcomed and it's just great. But as you say there is a pack away setting with things that are 30, 40 years old.

Dr Sue Allingham: And other users of the hall don't treat things respectfully.

Kathy Brodie: Yes. So that initial take on the emotional environment is very important. Once you've done that how do we then work on that to make sure that it is a good emotional environment, how do we take those emotional environments that may be are suffering how do we then improve those?

Dr Sue Allingham: I often have to get teams together and sometimes there's frank talking that goes on, which I'm sure you've had to experience before. Earlier on, before we started, I was telling you a bit about my Tai chi background. And I do some work with people very basic stuff, because I'm not a Tai Chi teacher but about taking time for yourself.

Because with the best will in the world, when you're working with young children you are flat out the whole time. And sometimes you are not feeling great, either physically or mentally. And it shows. However if you went and took yourself away just quietly and sat on your own and did some breathing or just switched off for a minute you'd come back into that room feeling more refreshed. It doesn't take long.

I've done breathing work with people on courses before now, just take that five minutes. And also to start looking at things a little bit more objectively. Sometimes we get very closed in on things. Some people get very het up and tied up with the routines of the day. Oh it's 10:30, we have to be doing this; it's 11 o'clock, we must be doing that. So we unpick some rules and routines and look at actually, do we really need to do that, when that time is? And because it's always said on our day plan that we have story after snack or that table goes here. Does it really need to?

There's several reasons why my consultancy is called 'out of the box'. That is one of them just because its always been done like that, doesn't mean it has to be done like that now. And sometimes it's the management of the setting, through just habit that causes the tension.

Kathy Brodie: And sometimes as with the very best intentions as well. And because it's worked for that particular cohort of children, because that worked last year, then we repeat the same things, we're going to get the same outcomes but that reflective practice is so valuable.

Dr Sue Allingham: It's not easy for people. And sometimes it takes a lot of talking to people. And a lot of gaining trust with people.

Kathy Brodie: So I think that's a really good place for people to start. I think that's a fantastic top tip already, just stepping back taking those few minutes, have a little bit deep breathing and to reflect on what is going on.

And maybe standing in a corner for a minute and having a look round the room and saying what's actually happening here today? What is going on here? I think that's a great place to start with the well-being and with those sort of Scales. And we've already said about how we need to get some of that foundation in place. What are the sort of challenges are they when they when you are using the Leuven scales?

Dr Sue Allingham: Well a major challenge - well, there are two really - one is that they're put out there as I said earlier, they are on a lot of assessment tools and people use them without really understanding what they're for or what they actually look like. The other one is personal opinion.

Now when I run training courses, I problematize, if you like, the idea. And every so often, all the way through, I say what will stand in the way of doing it? And one of them I throw up there is people's opinions of things. We all know about looking at children with a halo and horns effects in our heads you know the beautiful blonde little girl is obviously a well behaved well looked after. Completely happy in her own soul body thing and a dirty grimy runny nose little boy is clearly not, whereas, it could be completely the other way around.

That's why you really need to understand what well-being actually looks like. In a sort of mental way rather than a physical way. And not just think, well he's clearly got good well-being because he is involved in that. But what does involvement mean? Does it mean he's doing it because I told him to?

So it's a personal opinion thing and I think that's the biggest biggest challenge with all of this stuff is the subjective thing. Unless you have a whole team understanding. So just because he'll spent 10 minutes doing that puzzle because you told him to, doesn't mean he's highly involved in that puzzle. You've got to really get it, and really understand it.

Unless you physically have done some work around this is a whole team and got a whole team feeling about what well-being is, therefore what involvement is, you're going to have, I don't know, 10, 12 different people in a team not really getting it and saying well he's obviously very involved in his work, but he's not. Or on the flip side of that. We all hear people talking about children flitting from activity to activity, which is not necessarily a bad thing, but you really need to watch it to understand what's happening.

Kathy Brodie: Yes we have that understanding of why it is going from activity. What is their thinking process? I always think it be a lot easier if we could actually see inside their heads but we can't do that!

Dr Sue Allingham: We can't do that, but we can make very informed thinking for ourselves. You hit on a really good one - flitting - because so many times I've heard and I've seen video clips used on training a long time ago, towards Foundation Stage profile and moderation. And there were several people in the room that watched this child on video clip moving from thing to thing all the way around the room and were very concerned about him but my colleague and I watched it and we weren't concerned because of the way we felt - it's very difficult on a video clip where you don't know the children - but we overlaid a completely different story on it.

And we weren't concerned about him.

So that's that is the major challenge when using the Scales is not making those snap decisions.

Kathy Brodie: I think they're linked very closely with tuning into the children understanding our children. You know, this child might constantly be highly involved, but today is involved in nothing. That might sound the warning bells, even though that might be quite normal behaviour for a different child so that tuning in is also quite important in understanding the children. When you're using those.

Dr Sue Allingham: Yes. Because if you notice a child goes off for some reason then you need to follow through and see. It might just be that they've got a tummy ache that day.

Kathy Brodie: That's part of the well-being, that you've got to understand where they are in the well-being and maybe if the involvement scales are looking a bit strange - that child has dropped back in their well-being scales - and saying "Right let's just take this back and have a look see where we're at well-being wise first".

Dr Sue Allingham: And I think you've hit on a good point there as well. The Leuven scales are a tool to be used. They aren't to be used the whole time because they lose their efficacy, if you're using them all the time for everything. They are a very useful tool when you don't understand something. Or for a specific group of children that you're working with.

You can use them for a whole cohort of children if you want to, but then when you've done that initial assessment, if you like, then pull out a few you're concerned about working with. And then if a child suddenly does go off, like you say, and their involvement suddenly becomes different, use again. So that's a really important point about using them is that you use them to suit an appropriate need.

Kathy Brodie: And I think that's actually essential to emphasize because I don't think that's happening. I think at the moment it's sort of almost a box isn't it that you fill in or what's the number that we need to put in this box.

Dr Sue Allingham: And it's just is meaningless. And that's what concerns me about some of the electronic record keeping observation tools that you use on ipads and things. I am familiar with some of them that actually have a box for ticking off the well-being and involvement scales. And that's defeating the purpose. Because you shouldn't need to be using them all the time.

Kathy Brodie: It's again it's understanding the assessment tools that you've been given, same as the profile and anything else that people are using around the world. I know that having spoken to many people in different countries that they have similar kind of issues that they get given a set of guidelines and then suddenly - almost like common sense goes out the window doesn't it? This is what the guidelines say so this is what we've got to work towards. You need that reflective practice again.

Dr Sue Allingham: Then people suddenly say "Well we've got all these assessments, all the paperwork to do all this and all that" and we think well, no! And actually it's very pertinent with Leuven Scales work particularly, because you just end up with a set of numbers on a piece of paper every few weeks and it tells you nothing.

Kathy Brodie: Yes it doesn't give you that whole picture at all about the child. It's very important that we know what order to use them in, how we use them and to actually understand them and as you say I think that takes training. I don't think you can just print them off and take them in. I think you do need is that bit of support and training on that, at least reading around it if nothing else.

Dr Sue Allingham: I absolutely agree with you. I've got a bit of background and I do a lot of training in it. From my point of view talking with other people and coming to agreements about things is very important which is what I meant about team understanding. You can't just give somebody a piece of paper with the descriptions and a chart of five numbers. You have to really sit down and look at how Ferre describes what the levels look like and how the children feel in the case studies and its really important stuff.

Kathy Brodie: Yes and have that understanding as a team as to what's going on as well. And everybody brings their own experiences as well as their knowledge of their children. So, we all have that little piece of the puzzle, about that particular child because we've all seen something different. And as I said before we all interpret things differently as well you know your level of risky play can be very different to somebody else's.

Dr Sue Allingham: Absolutely. That's a very good one to pick on.

Kathy Brodie: I've come across this a few times and that team cohesion is so important as you say for the emotional well-being. Wow, there's loads of tips already. So Sue, what would your absolute top tip or top strategy be for practitioners, if they are wanting to work with the Leuven scales? What would your top tips be?

Dr Sue Allingham: I think we probably covered them already but my absolute top tip will be first of all get a decent book written by Ferre Laevers and Julia Moons - one or the other or both - from Leuven university.

Get some good background on it.

And then, if you can somewhere find some training on it and

obviously I can do it, if people want to take me, but get a good background on it. Local authorities run training, you can get packs with videos in, which are fine. I know you can buy those through various places.

Be wary of what you read, is all I will say because social media and the internet are wonderful places, but if you want to know about this stuff go back to source and read proper research documents. There's a lot of stuff out there that people write about and blog about and do stuff about that doesn't take it back to source and give you a proper briefing on it. So I think that's probably the toppest tip if you like.

So you've got to go into this thing with an open mind and understand - sometimes when I run training on this I get people talking about how they feel when they arrive and I always have to give the health warning that this isn't a counselling session! I've had on one notable occasion somebody started telling me an awful story and I had to say "I'm really sorry but if you need to talk I'm happy to talk afterwards in a private capacity. But this isn't the time to share this".

But it is about understanding how we feel about things and then really looking at how the children feel. So go to source and be ready to be reflexive about yourself.

Kathy Brodie: You do hold team trainings through your 'out of the box' consultancy. I'm a big fan of a whole team trainings, I think they are the way to go. There's nothing more demoralizing as a single practitioner coming back from a great course and you're the only one that's evangelizing, you need to have everybody on board.

Dr Sue Allingham: Absolutely. And I do a lot of teams I love working with Nursery teams and things because, as you say, they need to have the whole package don't they?

Kathy Brodie: So that's been absolutely marvellous. The other thing I know that you're very involved with that I just want to touch on briefly before we go is Keeping Early Years Unique campaign. Tell people who maybe've been hiding under a rock and have not seen this, can you tell them a little bit about what it is.

Dr Sue Allingham: There are several thousand people already involved in this. Basically, in a nut shell, nearly two years [i.e. 2015] ago a wonderful lady called Elaine Bennett, two years ago come Easter decided she'd had enough of the way the Early Years was going in the world, she is an Early Years teacher herself and contacted a few people that she knew names of, myself being one of them, to say would I be interested in being part of the Facebook page, Keeping Early Years Unique KEYU. And, I think the word is exponential, it's grown exponentially since she kicked it off and it's really wonderful. There were six of us behind it. There's myself, Kym Scott, Kathryn Solly, Anna Ephgrave, Ruth Moore and Leah Morris and we've just done our third conference - we've done London, Leeds and Bristol we're heading off to Dublin soon and we're doing Manchester and Birmingham.

Basically its about the key principles of Early Years. What it's not - and we're finding this a lot - it's not a specific way of doing things. People are seeing it as a method if you like. And is this the KEYU way. It's getting it back to basic principles.

So all of the founding fathers stuff, the key principles of Isaacs and Froebel we're bringing it all back, all key Early Years stuff. So we do work on interactions and management. Obviously my stuff has a lot about transitions and PSED key important early year stuff. So it's not as a method it's principles.

So if you haven't found Keeping Early Years Unique (KEYU) Facebook page yet, as you said they might have it under a rock, there's more than 20, 000 people on it now.

Kathy Brodie: Yes and it's very active as well as always new.

Dr Sue Allingham: It's highly active and there's always petitions to sign to Justine Greening about developmentally appropriate practice and most importantly, as far as I'm concerned as it goes to up to age 7. When I was first ever an Early Years co-ordinator, a hundred years ago, I was in charge of the infant department as well, as an early is co-ordinator and that seems to have slipped..

Kathy Brodie: It does and more and more so it seems almost to be certainly in England in the UK that the minute they get to school the whole idea of Early Years just disappears, even though they might only be four years old which is quite scary actually. The other thing I like about the Keeping Early Years Unique is that it doesn't matter whether you're in a Montessori setting or wherever, its just good practice.

Dr Sue Allingham: Not at all - childminders, everybody. It's Early Years principals, all the things that good Early Years practice is about.

Kathy Brodie: And you find a link to the Keeping Early Years Unique Facebook page on the Summit website here, so you can just click through and have a read. As I say there's always lots going on so go see what's happening on there now. And hopefully we'll see a Keeping Early Years Unique book at some point as well.

Dr Sue Allingham: There is one underway.

Kathy Brodie: I can't wait - that is going to be excellent, I'm really looking forward to that. Sue thank you so so much for joining us today. It's just been a revelation and I know that I'm going to be going back and having a look at some of my reading lists as well. And going back to source and getting some of that together I think for practitioners out there there's some really really sound advice.

Thank you so much for joining us today in the Early Years websites.

Dr Sue Allingham: Thanks Kathy, it was a pleasure.

CHAPTER 16

THE LINKS BETWEEN PHYSICAL DEVELOPMENT AND PSED

Sally Goddard Blythe

Kathy Brodie: I'm absolutely thrilled to be joined by Sally Goddard Blythe, a well-known name everywhere. Sally is a director for the Institute for Neuro Physiological Psychology (INPP) International where she's worked since 1988. She's the author of many many books about the INPP method and child development and they include reflexes learning behaviour, the Well-balanced Child, What Babies and Children Need Attention, Balance and Coordination - The ABC of learning success (which is my personal favourite it's really good). Assessing Neuromotor Readiness for Learning and Neuromotor Immaturity in Children and Adults. Welcome to the Early Years Web Summit, Sally Goddard Blythe.

Sally Goddard Blythe: Thank you Kathy and thank you very much for inviting me.

Kathy Brodie: Oh it's a real pleasure. I can't wait to hear everything that you've got to say about INPP, but today we're going to be focussing on how understanding children's physical development underpins all their other development and specifically how the INPP method can help children. So first of all, could you just explain a bit about the basis for the Institute of Neuro Physiological Psychology methods please Sally?

Sally Goddard Blythe: Well this started out really in the 1970s as a quest to discover whether children who are presenting with symptoms of underachievement such as reading, writing and spelling problems and so on had underlying physical factors or problems that were contributing to the presenting difficulty, rather than just looking at the surface. Why is the child not reading writing and spelling? Shall we teach more of the same? Trying to find out if the mechanics were there to enable a child to be successful.

So at that time Peter Blythe, who started INPP, was a senior lecturer in Applied Education, at a college in Lancashire and he and one of his mature students decided to go into schools and carry out several tests to see whether there were physical problems. They looked at things like patterns of motor development laterality, which in those days was considered to be very important, eye movements and so on.

They found that the children who were not necessarily diagnosed actually as having problems, but who were underachieving, all had a profile where their physical abilities were less well-developed than the children who were achieving at or above expected levels.

So that was the sort of origin of it, which then led them into trying to develop methods, reliable methods, of assessing those physical factors and then - perhaps more importantly - was it possible to put together physical movement programmes that would put some of those problems right. So really in a nutshell that's pretty much what the INPP method still is today and that's where it came from.

But what I should probably add is that the assessment tools that are used have been taken directly from mainstream medicine. So if they were carried out by a physiotherapist, occupational therapist, paediatrician they should come up with the same results that we do, so that there is a degree of inter test reliability in the methods of assessment that are being used.

Kathy Brodie: And obviously very much based in that evidence. This is something that is been proven isn't it?

Sally Goddard Blythe: Yes. We have tried very hard, although we are not within the sort of medical modality, to make what we do acceptable in terms of the tools and methods that we use.

Kathy Brodie: And this is international as well. We're not just talking about England or even the UK. This is around the world now isn't it.

Sally Goddard Blythe: I think it was 14 plus countries last time I counted, Yes.

Kathy Brodie: So that shows if it actually works for all sorts of children, it's not just a particular context or a particular group of children this is actually something that's going to work across the board for most children isn't it?

Sally Goddard Blythe: Yes, that it's not socially or culturally dependent that it is to do with children's biological development rather than where they happen to have grown up.

Kathy Brodie: Which obviously gives it a lot more weight as well. Now you've written a lot. But as I say I'd like to focus a little bit on Attention, Balance and Coordination - the ABC of Learning Success. In this book you explain how early reflexes affect learning in behaviour. Can you explain a little bit about what an early reflex is and then how that goes on to affect learning behaviour please.

Sally Goddard Blythe: Okay it might take some time! There are two main groups of reflexes that develop in a child's early life. The first one is called primitive reflexes and these are reflexes which start to emerge during life in the womb, and should be fully present in a baby born at full term, so 40 weeks gestation and are active from birth but are then gradually inhibited or put to sleep by higher centres in the brain as connections to higher centres in the brain develop in the first six months of life, which they do very rapidly.

And at the same time as those early reflexes are being inhibited or integrated, they are gradually either replaced or transformed into a group of postural reactions which give a child, in a general sense, control of balance, coordination and so on in a gravity based environment at a subconscious level. So you don't have to think too much about how do you sit, how do you stand, how do you walk. The executive part of the brain says this is what I want to do and the lower centres will do that at a subconscious level.

We will all probably recognize some of these little reflexes. If you stroke down the side of a new-born baby's face, here, the head will turn and the mouth will open search or rooting for the breast or the bottle.

If you place something in the palm of their hands the thumb will come underneath and the fingers will grasp and the baby won't let go. And as supremely egotistical adults we say "Isn't that sweet. Baby wants to hang on to her". Well she actually has very little choice at this time. Now those little reflexes should become modified so that when something is placed either in the palm of their hand or between the thumb and forefinger at a later age the thumb no longer wants to come underneath. And the other fingers is to come on top. And the inhibition of that reflex means that a child can then form a good pincer grip and then have good control of a writing instrument.

But if traces of that reflex are still present as that child tries to place something between the thumb and forefinger, this is what the hand would like to do and it makes it very difficult to form the correct writing grip which then potentially can have an impact on a child's fine motor coordination skills later on. There's a lot in the press at the moment about pressure on 5 year olds being made to write and perhaps too many tests and so on. That's another issue.

But it does tie in with the whole issue of a child's physical readiness for the demands of the classroom that it's going to be placed in. If a child doesn't have those physical skills in place, whatever the age, then they are going to start to fail and underachieve, not because they don't have the intelligence to do so but because they can't control the mechanics involved in the tasks that support academic learning.

Kathy Brodie: That is actually a biological reflex isn't it. They're not being naughty or not trying. That's tied into their biologies.

Sally Goddard Blythe: Or their developmental readiness really.

Kathy Brodie: And that's really interesting. They still have the reflexes up to six months. So really even at six months if we're looking at babies starting to sit down and all this that's going on along with their primitive reflexes already isn't it.

Sally Goddard Blythe: Yes. This is a normal progression where one skill overlaps and overrides another. The two may be present for a period of time normally. And then the higher one should gradually take over and that's pretty much how we develop you know through all our Early Years and later years and so on. But for some reason in some children something just gets blocked somewhere and everything else develops as it should. But that specific skill can continue to be affected by the partial retention of one of those early reflexes.

Kathy Brodie: Right, so that would explain some of the learning in some of the other things that are going on physically. I know that you talk a little bit about how that might affect behaviour as well. Could you tie that together for me please.

Sally Goddard Blythe: Yes. I mean there is one reflex something called a symmetrical tonic neck reflex which emerges just before a baby is ready to creep on hands and knees.

If it tries to put its head up then the top half of the body will extend and the lower half of the body will flex. It puts its head down the top of the body flexes and the lower half of the body tries to extend. So what? If that is still present when you go to school and you have to learn to sit up straight, provided your head is looking straight ahead there's no problem, but if your head looks down and your arms want to collapse it makes it very difficult to continue to sit in an upright position.

It also means the upper and lower portion of the bodies are at odds with each other. They're wanting to do different things. It makes it very difficult to sit still for any length of time. So these are the children who become the fidgets, the ones who wrap their legs around the chair to try and remain stable. Don't want to sit still on story time when sitting on the carpet not because they're naughty but because they can't. So behaviour is the secondary outcome of an underlying physical immaturity and a specific skill.

Kathy Brodie: I'm just thinking now I've seen children writing with their head on their arms on the table. And again you say "oh sit up, sit up". And if they're unable to do that you in fact ask him something to do something very difficult there. That's absolutely fascinating, I hadn't considered it from a physical point of view at all. That's really interesting. And I'm assuming that's going to lead on to things like anxiety, stress. Could you could you just tell us a little bit about what might be the consequences of some of those things.

Sally Goddard Blythe: Well I think you've touched on it that if a child doesn't have the automatic control over physical skills they have to work at many of their tasks much harder than they should. A lot of thinking effort goes into making the body do what should have become an automatic ability. And so that thinking brain gets overloaded more quickly than someone who doesn't have those difficulties.

Therefore the threshold to stress is lower or you are starting to suffer from the effects of stress. So that can be one factor but we also see a different profile of problems in adults. We see our adult who suffer from agoraphobia, acute anxiety and panic disorder. Now there can be many exogenous reasons as to why those can develop. But there can also be inner reasons as well. So we know that the functioning of the balance mechanism is crucial to our sense, not only of physical stability, but emotional stability as well.

And that many of the physical symptoms associated with experience of anxiety can be induced by inappropriate or overstimulation of the balance mechanism and it's related sensory systems. So for example if you go on a rollercoaster it's fine if you enjoy it you get a real buzz from it, but if you don't you feel sick, you feel disorientated, you feel distressed. And so the margin between being someone who enjoys it and who doesn't like it is actually quite subtle and quite small.

So some of our adults are those who are the children with physical immaturities grown up. Their problems were not so severe that they were picked up as learning difficulty when they were younger, they got through the education system by working hard by being good students. And as the pressures build up, later on then they start to suffer from emotional stress, if they don't identify a physical cause for that stress.

That stress can become generalized and you can start to develop avoidance behaviours of which agoraphobia would be one example. Also recognizing there could be many other reasons for the development of agoraphobia. But often simply by carrying out an assessment on an adult and inducing the feelings associated with stress during part of the assessment, you can help them for 50 per cent of the way of being able to deal with it, because they said "Ah, now I understand if you've been able to make me feel like that simply by this simple test it shows that there is a reason for it" instead of it being something which is they are not in control of because they don't know what sets it off.

Kathy Brodie: Sometimes having that explanation as well, you need that explanation before you can start to move forward. You need to understand what is happening already. If that's been undiagnosed in childhood with younger children then that can manifest to all sorts of things as an adult. So what we need to do then is just take it right back. How can we spot this? How can we assess what's going on with children rather than all that something out. How can we assess what's happening?

Sally Goddard Blythe: I think that's my political soapbox until I retire! Way I go back in the 1980s when my eldest son first went to school, a school medical officer used to see all children for a pre-school test where they would ask them to stand on one leg, hop to one end of the room, pile some bricks, simple vision and hearing test. Those were then phased out, so by the time my second son went to school, which was only two years later, they were no longer done. They were phased out because it was said 'well if we identified problems at that time, we didn't necessarily have effective programs of intervention'. So rather than simply assessing for assessments sake those assessments were discarded.

But in actual fact they are incredibly useful and we have produced a simple screening test for teachers, clinicians, health practitioners to use. It's not a diagnostic test but it is a screening procedure which you can use with children from about four or five years of age and upwards to identify. Are there indications of physical immaturity still present in this child before they start school? And that can be used again throughout their school career as a way of identifying children who *may* have later difficulties but are at risk of having difficulties as a result of those little physical immaturities being present.

And the ideal to me would then be to make a referral to the appropriate agency or professional to then investigate it further or implement physical programs in school. So it's not actually rocket science to try and reduce the incidence of this and help a larger number of children to achieve and teachers to be effective in the job that they're doing.

Kathy Brodie: Yes absolutely. That's a really good point isn't it, if you're asking children to do something physically they're unable to do, then nobody wins. The teachers don't get good outcomes. Children don't get good outcomes. And you can use that screening from pre-school so that is age in the UK that's age four and five is that right upwards.

Sally Goddard Blythe: And then you can use a slightly different battery of tests at seven years of age, nine years of age, 11 and 13. Ideally there should be no child going through the system who is not picked up at the earliest possible stage to say "right, this child doesn't have any problems with intelligence or ability to learn. But there is a blockage or there is a barrier to their ability to show that" and we should be able to do, not in all cases, but in many cases do something about it.

Kathy Brodie: Yes. That screening is not only identifying that there is something, you also identify *what* that something is. And then you can set them presumably down a path of some sort to start to correct some of those things. So I'm going to guess here that, because every child develops differently, that that program is going to be different for every single child and that will be unique it's not just a one size fits all.

Sally Goddard Blythe: Yes and no, I mean it's always a problem of money isn't it.

So the individual program we have developed over many years is still only accessd through the private system. And it was in answer to that that way back in 1996 I put together a developmental movement program that could be used with an entire class of children in school on the basis of either a one day teaching course for teachers, although that's now been published so people can access it through the publication as well.

The idea is that all children in the class can go through the program, it is aimed at those that need it most. But what has surprised even us is that those children who didn't apparently need it at the outset seemed to gain some benefits in other skills such as playground, coordination, PE, ability to sit still for longer - just general physical readiness to be able to cope with the demands of the world in which they're going to live.

Kathy Brodie: How interesting, so you can do that with a whole group of children and as you say everybody benefits. There are no losers, you've gone right from the other end to a win-win all round haven't you.

Sally Goddard Blythe: Well we hope so. I mean there is always a need for ongoing research and ongoing re-evaluation. So the studies that we did are now a few years old, but there was one of particular interest in a Derbyshire school were they took one entire year group of children aged seven to eight, I think they were, 90 children.

All children were assessed on the physical test to begin with and educational measures. They put one class of children through the school based INPP program, one class through general movements for the same time period each day, and the third class did only what was part of the National Curriculum Physical Education. And they reassessed them on physical tests and educational measures at the end.

What they found was that the children who did an extra 10 minutes of daily exercise of any kind made twice as much improvement as the children who did no extra exercise, which is interesting.

But they made only half as much as the children who did specific developmental movements that were aimed at trying to put these underlying problems right.

So, it's an old piece of research. It wasn't a very large set of numbers but it was interesting in that it suggests that daily physical movement of any kind is valuable but targeting it more specifically at the needs of the group that you're using is likely to be more effective. And I would like to see sort of on-going research really following up on that with larger numbers.

Kathy Brodie: And that's amazing, not talking about having to send them away or that's just something that any school could tap in to that could put in place. Obviously there's going to be some training of teachers and you need to know how to do the course but you're not talking about rocket science here is very easily applied.

Sally Goddard Blythe: You are accessing a large number of children or providing something for a large number of children for very little cost. Really once you start to use it it's a class based program. There will always be children within that group who ideally should have something devise more specifically for them. But it's a great deal better than nothing and perhaps not as perfect as it could be.

Kathy Brodie: It is a fantastic place to start isn't it. So what sorts of activities would you advise would be particularly beneficial for children and what type of things are you talking about.

Sally Goddard Blythe: It depends on the age of the children that you're targeting.

Movements that involve stimulation and practice of balance are generally incredibly useful. Balance I often describe as the forgotten sense. You know we talk about vision and hearing and touch and taste and smell and so on but in actual fact with the exception of taste and smell every one of those other sensory systems actually has to work in cooperation with the balance mechanism to give us a stable perception. So if there is an underlying problem in the functioning of balance it will speak through difficulties in processing information in other sensory systems so by working with balance. You work at the core or the foundation level.

So, it's movement, making sure children have plenty of movement opportunities throughout the day and that there's movement opportunities start from their level of ability rather than higher than their level of ability. So they are succeeding and building upwards rather than trying to drag a child up from the top down. I know that's sort of very general description but it's difficult to give you specifics.

I can tell you what our movement programs are based on. They take children back in time developmentally to replicate movements they should have made and mastered when they were very much younger, long before they started school. The theory being that you can put that vocabulary back in but again starting from the bottom upwards building from the roots up towards the top rather than from the branches down.

Kathy Brodie: So are you talking about as basic as crawling?

Sally Goddard Blythe: The school program takes nine months of daily exercises to get the children ready to crawling and creeping at the end of the program. That's one of the major differences between our program and perhaps many other well known motor training programs that they will start at perhaps the crawling and creeping, cross pattern movement stage of development.

And we say yes, that's fine and it will work for many, many

children. But there are others who, actually this has never become an integrated function. And you need to put earlier pieces of motor vocabulary in place first to enable those then to become an automatic and integrated skill later on.

Kathy Brodie: Because I think I read somewhere, probably in your books, that crawling is actually quite sophisticated isn't it because you have to get all the movements in in synchronicity, it is quite complicated.

Sally Goddard Blythe: Babies are very clever with the things that they can do and they learn to do. And the assumption is that if you put that in, then it will all come into place - and for some children it will. It depends on their individual level of difficulty was whether they need to go earlier and whether they need to go deeper or whether a more general motor training program will be the answer.

Kathy Brodie: So if we're thinking about practitioners who may be watching that are working in the baby room who are working with some of the smallest babies. The idea that once they can walk I think there's a temptation to make them walk. "Come on stand up, stop crawling". That, in fact, you should be allowing them to crawl maybe.

Sally Goddard Blythe: Yes I mean it's been suggested that the process of crawling on hands and knees trains eye movements from side to side, following one hand and then the other at the same visual distance that a child will use for reading and writing later on, so that it is a precursor to a more sophisticated eye tracking movements later.

And so it's the old thing of don't try to run before you learn to walk, don't try and learn to walk, before you learn to crawl. Not every child goes through crawling but to embrace each of those stages as being important building blocks for later higher skills and not to try and rush your children through those early stages.

Kathy Brodie: Yes absolutely I think that's a really strong message that children should still be crawling through tunnels, should be doing all the really what we might consider basic physical things, because that's the foundation on which everything else is then built.

Are there any other activities maybe for the pre-school children that maybe practitioners can be doing, not necessarily in preparation for school but to aid the children in that transition.

Sally Goddard Blythe: Movement and song, and movement and music together. It is often forgotten that written language developed from an oral culture in which knowledge was passed on through the telling of stories. The singing of songs, ballads and all those sorts of things. And I often describe this as the music of language long before children learn to differentiate all the individual sounds within a word, they pick up the stream, the intonation, the timing and so on all the sort of nonverbal aspects of language and those we learn through lullabies, nursery rhymes listening to stories, real physical, social engagement. So it's not the same when you sit in front of a screen or you play with a game because that is pre-programmed. It doesn't listen to what the child has to say.

And there's some wonderful work done by Professor Colwyn Trevarthen and colleagues up at the University of Edinburgh, observing mother infant conversations or interaction and he shows how if a mother is talking to her baby using motherese and she sort of goes "lad Ed did a da" if she waits for a few seconds the baby will look. It will process that and then it will give a perfect answering phrase. It'll go something much like "la da did id da" If she moves on too fast, baby can't cope with that and it gives up. Or if somebody comes in and interrupts before the babies had a chance to do it, it looks as if to say "Don't you understand? You need to wait for me." So it is this what we call paralanguage. It's gesture precedes spoken language just as vocalization.

And these are all the things that young children need to practice and learn and experience in the Early Years. And so the games of yesteryear are still incredibly important. And it's not that I'm a Luddite and says that all technology should be eliminated but technology is actually for us when we're older.

It's not how we were designed to develop as mammals and biologically in a physical world. We still need that experience to create the building blocks for later life.

Kathy Brodie: Yes I have to say some of my happiest memories is playing out Ring a Roses, all those lovely games that you play outside where you can really get a good level of movement as well as all the language it's built in with that. So that's really simple again isn't it? That's circle games outside, that's games indoors. Does it have a physical element to them? Doesn't cost anything you just need to maybe think about what you're presenting for the child and what you're giving to them there.

That's really great advice thank you very much. What if we do have practitioners out there who maybe have concerns about their children that are thinking "You know what, I think there's something that's not that's not gelling quite right here". What would you suggest that they do?

Sally Goddard Blythe: Again it depends a little bit on the age of the child and the type of problems they're concerned about. We developed many years ago a screening questionnaire. Once again it is only a screening device not a diagnostic tool but that has been published several times in various books and articles.

Practitioners can access that through contact with us or our website and it gives them an indication if there are enough factors in early development to suggest that neuro-motor immaturity may be one factor in this child's presenting problems.

It also has an auditory section to see whether auditory processing difficulties may be a contributing factor. It also has a very simple indications for signs of sort of biochemical nutritional factors that may be playing a part in perhaps a child's behavioural problems.

That's something that they can access, they can use it with together with the parent to see whether it's flagging up concerns and then on the basis of how highly a child has scored, it will give them an indication as to which direction they might suggest that parent follows.

Kathy Brodie: That's a whole suite of things, is it's a whole range of things and it just highlights how children develop holistically but also that sometimes it's not as simple as we think it might be at the beginning.

I know that you do training for practitioners and for teachers and for parents as well could you tell us a little bit about the sorts of training courses that you do please?

Sally Goddard Blythe: Well we have three levels. We have a screening one day course for clinicians and health practitioners in screening for signs of this. Some of whom will then want to go on to learn how to do it for many others. All they need to know is how to identify it and then to pass on either within the medical service or other agencies where the family can get extra help.

We then have a one day course for teachers in the use of the screening test. They can use in school and how to implement the class based program that we talked about.

And then we have a one year course for professionals who need to have an existing qualification in either education, medicine, psychology or an allied field to access that course. But in how to learn how to become practitioners who will do the assessments and supervise individual programs with children.

Kathy Brodie: That is as deep as you'd like to go with this if you did a whole year course you could then roll that out. I think that be fascinating for teachers as well to come along and learn how you can implement this in your setting, of course that that's lifelong, isn't it, once you've got those good habits.

Sally Goddard Blythe: Once the school has got it within the system, then that can be rolled out year upon year with, ideally, it's year three group is the best age to do. It can be done with other age groups at that school that has it as a tool in place which can come become part and parcel of their ethos.

Kathy Brodie: I just think that would be absolutely excellent that would be massively worthwhile investment.

It's been absolutely fascinating talking with you all about the work that you do and some of the really quite simple things that we can implement.

Also changing the way that we think about how children learn and how they behave in unpicking that a little bit that's been really interesting. Thank you so much for joining us today on The Early Years Web Summit Sally Goddard Blythe.

Sally Goddard Blythe: Thank you.